Welcome

The first quilt that many quilters make is a baby quilt, and through the years, many quilters continue to make quilts for the babies of their family and friends. Soft quilts and babies just seem to go together.

Whether you are an expectant mother awaiting the arrival of your baby or a grandmother looking for just the right quilt design for a special baby, you'll find in this collection of creative quilts and projects just what you want to stitch for your next project.

Baby quilts are irresistible. Some are cute and some are lacy. Some are in bright colors and others are in pastels. Some are pieced, some are appliquéd and some are a combination of techniques.

In addition to baby quilts, other popular items to make for baby are practical bibs, changing mats and burp pads, attractive wall quilts, fun play mats and photo frames, helpful bulletin boards, a variety of toys and a handy stroller pack.

If you are decorating a nursery for a new baby, look for the chapter of adorable baby sets. In addition to precious baby quilts, there is an entire nursery of projects to make that match the quilts in this section. Select your favorite set and decorate the entire nursery with the same theme.

As you stitch something special for Baby, we know that every stitch will be filled with love for that precious little one. Quilting and babies do go together

Happy quilting!

Jeanne Stauffer

Sandra L. Hatch

Contents

Irresistible Baby Quilts

Baby quilts are so much fun to make. Because of their small size they are quick and easy; they are the baby gift everyone adores.

Sweet Dreams

Design by Julie Weaver

Soft yellow and green combine with white in this pretty star-design quilt.

PROJECT SPECIFICATIONS

Skill Level: Beginner
Quilt Size: 40" x 52"
Block Size: 6" x 6"
Number of Blocks: 35

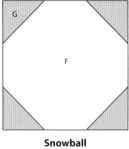

Snowball
6" x 6" Block
Make 17

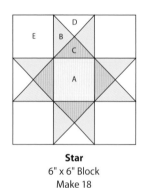

Star
6" x 6" Block
Make 18

FABRIC Measurements based on 43" usable fabric width.	#STRIPS & PIECES	CUT	#PIECES	SUBCUT
⅝ yard yellow check	3	3¼" x 43"	36	3¼" B squares
	2	1½" x 32½" I		
	2	1½" x 42½" H		
⅔ yard medium green dot	2	3¼" x 43"	18	3¼" C squares
	5	2½" x 43"	68	2½" G squares
1¼ yards white print	2	3¼" x 43"	18	3¼" D squares
	5	2½" x 43"	72	2½" E squares
	3	6½" x 43"	17	6½" F squares
1¼ yards light green print	2	4½" x 40½" K		
	3	4½" x 43" J		
	5	2¼" x 43" binding		
	18	2½" A squares with motif centered		
Backing		46" x 58"		

SUPPLIES

- Batting 46" x 58"
- Neutral color all-purpose thread
- Quilting thread
- Basic sewing tools and supplies

COMPLETING THE STAR BLOCKS

Step 1. Draw a diagonal line from corner to corner on the wrong side of each B square.

Step 2. Pair a B square with a C square with right sides together; stitch ¼" on each side of the marked line as shown in Figure 1.

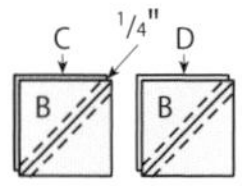

Figure 1

Step 3. Cut apart on the marked line to complete two B-C units as shown in Figure 2; press seams toward C. Repeat with remaining C squares and B to make 36 B-C units.

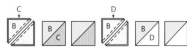

Figure 2

Step 4. Repeat Steps 2 and 3 with B and D squares, again referring to Figures 1 and 2 to make 36 B-D units.

Step 5. Draw a diagonal line across the previously stitched seam on the wrong side of each B-C unit as shown in Figure 3.

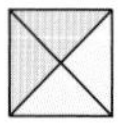

Figure 3 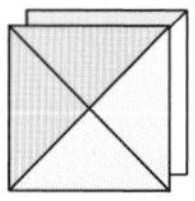   **Figure 4**

Step 6. Place a marked B-C unit right sides together with a B-D unit with opposite fabrics touching as shown in Figure 4.

Step 7. Stitch ¼" on each side of the marked line as shown in Figure 5. Cut apart on the drawn line to make two B-C-D units referring to Figure 6.

Figure 5   **Figure 6**

Step 8. To complete one Star block, sew a B-C-D unit to opposite sides of A to make the center row as shown in Figure 7; press seams toward A.

Figure 7

Step 9. Sew E to opposite sides of two B-C-D units to make the top and bottom rows referring to Figure 8; press seams toward E.

Figure 8

Step 10. Sew the center row between the top and bottom rows to complete one Star block; press seams away from the center row.

Step 11. Repeat Steps 8–10 to complete 18 Star blocks.

COMPLETING THE SNOWBALL BLOCKS
Step 1. Mark a diagonal line from corner to corner on the wrong side of each G square.

Step 2. Place a G square on each corner of F and stitch on the marked lines as shown in Figure 9.

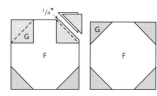

Figure 9

Step 3. Trim seams to ¼" and press G to the right side to complete one Snowball block.

Step 4. Repeat Steps 2 and 3 to complete 17 Snowball blocks.

COMPLETING THE QUILT

Step 1. Join three Star blocks with two Snowball blocks to make an X row as shown in Figure 10; press seams toward Snowball blocks. ***Note:** If A squares have a directional motif, be sure to arrange the blocks with the motif in the right direction.* Repeat to make four X rows.

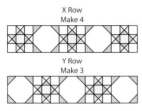

Figure 10

Step 2. Join three Snowball blocks with two Star blocks to make a Y row, again referring to Figure 10; press seams toward the Snowball blocks. Repeat to make three Y rows.

Step 3. Join the X and Y rows referring to the Placement Diagram for positioning; press seams in one direction.

Step 4. Sew an H strip to opposite long sides and I strips to the top and bottom of the pieced center; press seams toward H and I strips.

Step 5. Join the J strips on short ends to make one long strip; press seams open. Subcut strip into two 44½" J strips.

Step 6. Sew a J strip to opposite long sides and K strips to the top and bottom of the pieced center to complete the pieced top; press seams toward J and K strips.

Step 7. Finish the quilt referring to the Finishing Instructions on page 173. ●

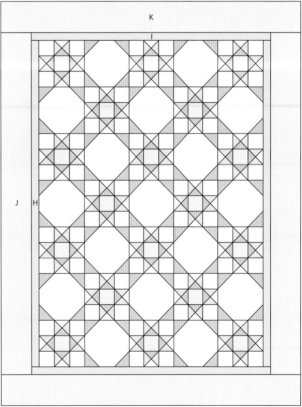

Sweet Dreams
Placement Diagram 40" x 52"

Under the Sea

Design by Julie Weaver

Showcase a whimsical fish print for a room decorated in an under-the-sea theme.

PROJECT SPECIFICATIONS
Skill Level: Beginner
Quilt Size: 40" x 40"
Block Size: 9" x 9"
Number of Blocks: 9

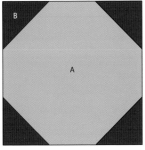

Snowball
9" x 9" Block
Make 5

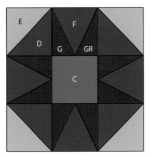

Star
9" x 9" Block
Make 4

FABRIC Measurements based on 42" usable fabric width	#STRIPS & PIECES	CUT	#PIECES	SUBCUT
⅓ yard green dot	1	3⅞" x 42"	8	3⅞" E squares
	2	1½" x 42"	8	9½" H pieces
½ yard red multicolored dot	2	3½" x 42"	20	3½" B squares
			4	1½" J squares
	1	3½" x 42" G		
	1	1½" x 42"	4	9½" I pieces
⅔ yard blue underwater print	5	9½" x 9½" A squares with motifs centered		
⅞ yard fish print	4	4½" C squares with fish motif centered		
	2	5" x 29½" K		
	2	5" x 38½" L		
⅞ yard blue swirl	1	3½" x 42" F		
	1	3⅞" x 42"	8	3⅞" D squares
	2	1½" x 38½" M		
	2	1½" x 40½" N		
	5	2¼" x 42" binding		
Backing		46" x 46"		

SUPPLIES

• Batting 46" x 46"
• Neutral color all-purpose thread
• Quilting thread
• Basic sewing tools and supplies

COMPLETING THE SNOWBALL BLOCKS
Step 1. Draw a diagonal line from corner to corner on the wrong side of each B square.

Step 2. Place a B square right sides together on each corner of A and stitch on the marked line as shown in Figure 1.

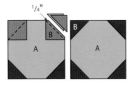

Figure 1

Step 3. Trim seams to ¼" and press B to the right side, again referring to Figure 1, to complete one Snowball block.

Step 4. Repeat Steps 2 and 3 to complete five Snowball blocks.

COMPLETING THE STAR BLOCKS

Step 1. Draw a diagonal line from corner to corner on the wrong side of each E square.

Step 2. Place an E square right sides together with a D square and stitch ¼" on each side of the marked line as shown in Figure 2; press open with seam toward E to complete two D-E units, again referring to Figure 2. Repeat to make 16 D-E units.

Figure 2

Step 3. Cut F and G pieces from the F and G strips referring to Figure 3.

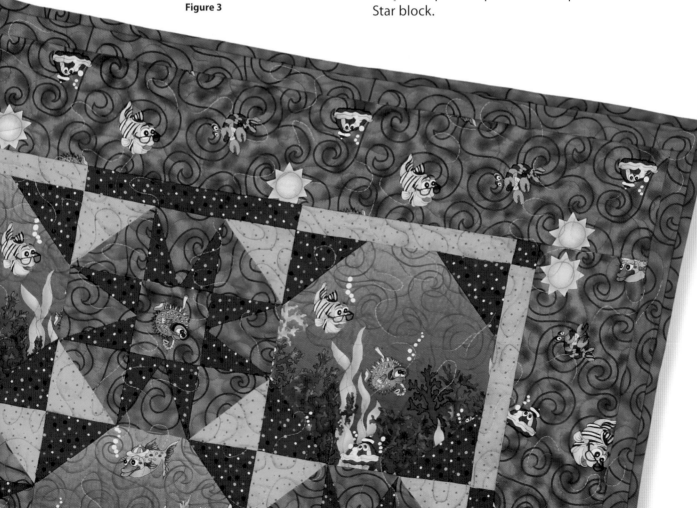

Figure 3

Step 4. Sew G and GR to F to make an F-G unit as shown in Figure 4; repeat to make 16 F-G units.

Figure 4

Step 5. To complete one Star block, sew an F-G unit to opposite sides of C to make the center row as shown in Figure 5; press seams toward C.

Figure 5

Step 6. Sew a D-E unit to opposite sides of an F-G unit to complete the top row; press seams toward D-E units. Repeat to make the bottom row.

Step 7. Sew the top and bottom rows to the center row to complete one Star block.

Step 8. Repeat Steps 5–7 to complete one Star block.

COMPLETING THE QUILT

Step 1. Join one Star block with two Snowball blocks to make an X row as shown in Figure 6; press seams toward Snowball blocks. Repeat to make two X rows.

X Row
Make 2

Figure 6

Step 2. Join one Snowball block with two Star blocks to make a Y row as shown in Figure 7; press seams toward Snowball block.

Y Row
Make 1

Figure 7

Step 3. Sew the Y row between the two X rows to complete the pieced center; press seams in one direction.

Step 4. Join one I strip with two H strips to make an H-I row as shown in Figure 8; press seams toward I strips. Repeat to make four H-I rows.

Figure 8

Step 5. Sew an H-I row to opposite sides of the pieced center; press seams toward H-I rows.

Step 6. Sew a J square to each end of the remaining H-I rows to make an H-I-J row, again referring to Figure 8; press seams toward I strips.

Step 7. Sew an H-I-J row to the top and bottom of the pieced center; press seams toward the H-I-J rows.

Step 8. Sew K strips to opposite sides and L strips to the top and bottom of the pieced center; press seams toward K and L strips.

Step 9. Sew M strips to opposite sides and N strips to the top and bottom of the pieced center; press seams toward M and N strips to complete the pieced top.

Step 10. Finish the quilt referring to the Finishing Instructions on page 173. ●

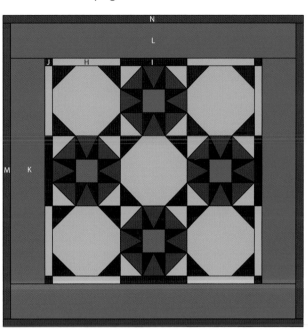

Under the Sea
Placement Diagram 40" x 40"

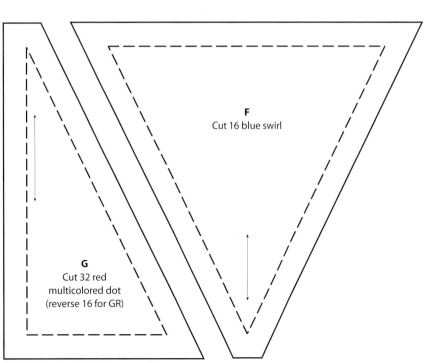

F
Cut 16 blue swirl

G
Cut 32 red multicolored dot (reverse 16 for GR)

Sleepy Kitty Nap Quilt

Design by Connie Rand

This quilt comes complete with kitties to help your little one get to sleep at naptime.

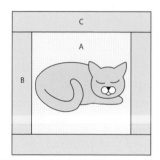

Sleepy Kitty
8" x 8" Block
Make 4 each blue,
green, pink & yellow

PROJECT SPECIFICATIONS

Skill Level: Beginner
Quilt Size: 41" x 41"
Block Size: 8" x 8"
Number of Blocks: 16

COMPLETING THE BLOCKS

Step 1. Trace kitty shapes on the paper side of the fusible web referring to pattern for number to cut; cut out shapes leaving a margin around each one.

Step 2. Fuse head, nose/mouth and body shapes to the wrong side of fabrics as directed on patterns. Cut out shapes on marked lines; remove paper backing.

Step 3. Fold A squares in quarters and crease to mark centerlines.

Step 4. Center each kitty on an A square in numerical order and fuse in place. Mark eyes and tail on each kitty with a chalk pencil.

Step 5. Cut (16) 5" x 6" rectangles fabric stabilizer; pin to the wrong side of each A square behind kitty motifs.

FABRIC Measurements based on 42" usable fabric width.	#STRIPS & PIECES	CUT	#PIECES	SUBCUT
⅛ yard each 4 coral prints		Appliqué pieces as per patterns		
¼ yard each blue and green tonals	1	5" x 32½" D each		
¼ yard each yellow and pink tonals	1	5" x 41½" E each		
⅜ yard each pink, yellow and green prints	4	1½" x 42" each	8	6½" B strips each
	1	2¼" x 42" binding each	8	8½" C strips each
½ yard blue print	4	1½" x 42"	8	6½" B strips
			8	8½" C strips
	2	2¼" x 42" binding		
¾ yard white tonal	3	6½" x 42" Appliqué pieces as per pattern	16	6½" A squares
Backing		47" x 47"		

SUPPLIES

- Batting 47" x 47"
- Neutral color all-purpose thread
- Quilting thread
- Coral rayon thread to match appliqué
- 1¼ yards 18"-wide fusible web
- 1¼ yards fabric stabilizer
- Fine-point permanent black marker
- Basic sewing tools and supplies and chalk pencil

Step 6. Machine satin-stitch around the kitties and on eye and tail lines using coral thread. Fill in details on nose with fine-point permanent black marker; remove fabric stabilizer.

Step 7. Select two each same-color B and C strips. Sew B to each side of an appliquéd A square and add C to the top and bottom referring to the block drawing to complete one Sleepy Kitty block; press seams toward B and C strips.

Step 8. Repeat Step 7 to complete four each blue, green, pink and yellow Sleepy Kitty blocks.

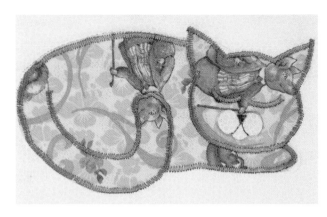

COMPLETING THE QUILT

Step 1. Arrange and join the blocks in four rows of four blocks each referring to the Placement Diagram for positioning of colors; press seams in adjoining rows in opposite directions.

Step 2. Join the rows to complete the pieced center; press seams in one direction.

Step 3. Sew D strips to opposite sides and E strips to the top and bottom of the pieced center to complete the pieced top referring to the Placement Diagram for color placement; press seams toward strips.

Step 4. Finish the quilt referring to the Finishing Instructions on page 173. ●

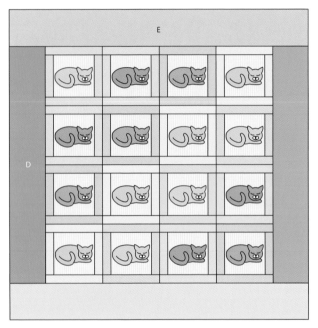

Sleepy Kitty Nap Quilt
Placement Diagram 41" x 41"

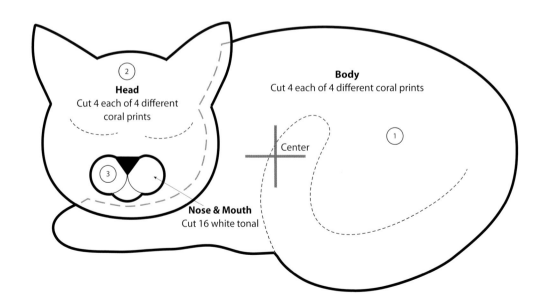

Head
Cut 4 each of 4 different coral prints
②

Body
Cut 4 each of 4 different coral prints
①

Center

Nose & Mouth
Cut 16 white tonal
③

Comfy Corners Play Quilt

Design by Linda Miller

Soft and cuddly, this quilt made with a combination of cottons and Minkee fabrics is perfect for Baby.

Comfy Corners
11" x 11" Block
Make 8

PROJECT SPECIFICATIONS

Skill Level: Beginner
Quilt Size: 54" x 54"
Block Size: 11" x 11"
Number of Blocks: 8

COMPLETING THE BLOCKS

Step 1. Sew the B strip between two C strips with right sides together along the length; press seams toward C strips.

Step 2. Subcut the B-C strip set into (16) 2½" B-C units as shown in Figure 1.

2½"

Figure 1

FABRIC Measurements based on 42" usable fabric width except as noted.	#STRIPS & PIECES	CUT	#PIECES	SUBCUT
¼ yard orange/ blue dot	2	2½" x 42" C strips		
⅝ yard blue animal print	2	7½" x 42"	8	7½" A squares
¾ yard 60"-wide light green Minkee	2	11½" x 60"	8	11½" D squares
¾ yard 60"-wide light blue Minkee	2 2	5½" x 44½" E 5½" x 54½" F		
1 yard blue/ green plaid	1 1 6	7½" x 42" B strip 7½" x 42" 2½" x 42" binding	16	2½" B rectangles
Backing		60" x 60" Minkee fabric		

SUPPLIES

- Batting 60" x 60"
- Neutral color all-purpose thread
- Quilting thread
- Basic sewing tools and supplies

Step 3. To complete one Comfy Corners block, sew a B rectangle to opposite sides of A; press seams toward B.

Step 4. Sew a B-C unit to the remaining sides of the A-B unit to complete one block referring to the block drawing; press seams toward the B-C unit.

Step 5. Repeat Steps 3 and 4 to complete eight Comfy Corners blocks.

COMPLETING THE QUILT

Step 1. Join two D squares with two Comfy Corners blocks to make a row referring to Figure 2; press seams toward D squares. Repeat to make four rows.

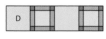

Figure 2

Step 2. Join the rows referring to the Placement Diagram to complete the pieced center; press seams in one direction.

Step 3. Sew an E strip to the top and bottom and F strips to opposite sides of the pieced center to complete the pieced top; press seams toward E and F strips.

Step 4. Finish the quilt referring to the Finishing Instructions on page 173. ●

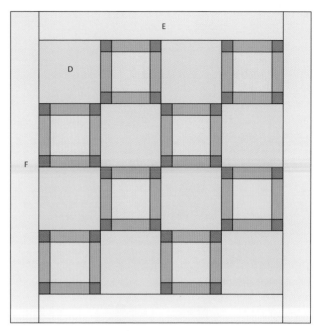

Comfy Corners Play Quilt
Placement Diagram 54" x 54"

Fun Fish Quilt

Design by Mary Ayres

Understated, simple designs carry the day in this easy-to-stitch fish-design quilt.

PROJECT SPECIFICATIONS
Skill Level: Beginner
Quilt Size: 31¼" x 37½"
Block Size: 6¼" x 6¼"
Number of Blocks: 10

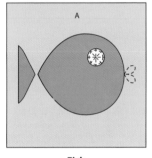

Fish
6¼" x 6¼" Block
Make 5

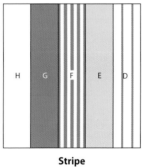

Stripe
6¼" x 6¼" Block
Make 5

FABRIC Measurements based on 42" usable fabric width.	#STRIPS & PIECES	CUT	#PIECES	SUBCUT
Scraps yellow, purple, pink, green and orange tonals		Appliqué pieces as per pattern		
⅓ yard each light and dark blue and narrow and wide stripe chambray	1	6¾" x 42"	5	6¾" squares each fabric for A, B, C and I
	1	1¾" x 42" strip each fabric for D, E, F and G		
½ yard white solid	1	6¾" x 42"	5	6¾" J squares
	1	1¾" x 42" H Appliqué pieces as per pattern		
Backing		33" x 39"		

SUPPLIES
- Batting 33" x 39"
- Neutral color all-purpose thread
- Quilting thread
- 1 skein bright blue embroidery floss
- 4 yards medium blue jumbo rickrack
- ⅜ yard 18"-wide fusible web
- Basic sewing tools and supplies and water-erasable marker

COMPLETING THE STRIPE BLOCKS
Step 1. Join the D, E, F, G and H strips with right sides together along length; press seams in one direction.

Step 2. Subcut the D–H strip set into five 6¾" Stripe blocks as shown in Figure 1.

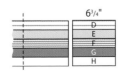

6¾"
D
E
F
G
H

Figure 1

COMPLETING THE FISH BLOCKS
Step 1. Trace appliqué shapes onto the paper side of the fusible web as directed on pattern for number to cut; cut out shapes, leaving a margin around each one.

Step 2. Fuse shapes to the wrong sides of the tonal scraps; cut out shapes on traced lines. Remove paper backing.

Step 3. Fold and crease each A square to find the center.

Step 4. Center and fuse a fish motif on A using creased lines and mark on pattern as guides for placement, placing fish so they go in different directions as shown in Figure 2. Fuse an eye on each fish.

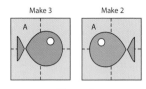

Figure 2

Step 5. Transfer lip shapes and eye design to A with a water-erasable marker using the pattern given.

Step 6. Using 2 strands of bright blue embroidery floss, stem-stitch around lips and around body, tail and eye shapes ⅛" from edges. Straight stitch lines from the eye center to the outside edges on top of the stem stitches to complete the blocks.

COMPLETING THE QUILT

Step 1. Arrange and join the completed blocks with the B, C, I and J squares to make six rows of five blocks each referring to the Placement Diagram for positioning of blocks; press seams in adjacent rows in opposite directions.

Step 2. Sew rickrack to the quilt top ¼" from the edge, beginning and ending in a corner.

Step 3. Using the quilt top as a pattern, trim backing and batting the same size.

Step 4. Pin batting to the wrong side and backing right sides together with the completed top; stitch all around on the stitching line holding the rickrack in place, leaving a 6" opening on one side.

Step 5. Trim batting close to stitching and trim corners.

Step 6. Turn right side out through the opening; press edges flat along seam.

Step 7. Press the opening seams ¼" to the wrong side and hand-stitch opening closed.

Step 8. Quilt as desired by hand or machine to complete the quilt. ●

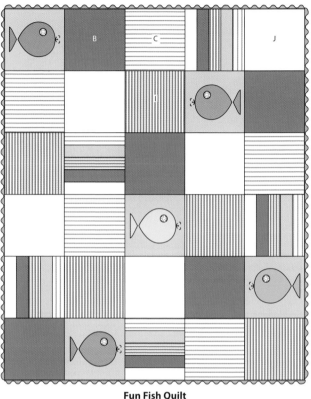

Fun Fish Quilt
Placement Diagram 31¼" x 37½"

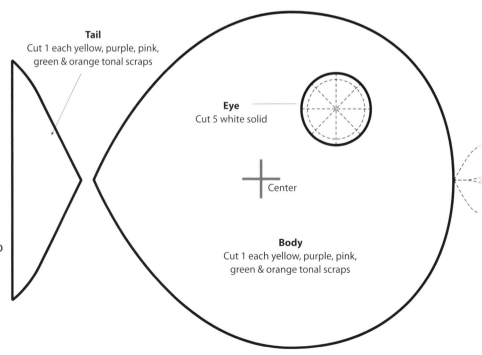

Tail
Cut 1 each yellow, purple, pink, green & orange tonal scraps

Eye
Cut 5 white solid

Center

Body
Cut 1 each yellow, purple, pink, green & orange tonal scraps

Cowboy Stars

Design by Lisa Moore

Start with a cowboy print and add some red and blue bandana-style prints, and you have a quilt fit for a real cowpoke!

PROJECT NOTE

To help with fussy-cutting the focus fabrics, tape a 3½" paper half-square triangle to the back of a 6½"-square clear ruler as shown in Figure 1. Place the ruler on the fabric to audition the motifs before cutting.

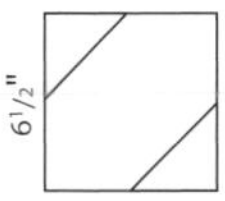

Figure 1

PROJECT SPECIFICATIONS

Skill Level: Intermediate
Quilt Size: 44" x 56"

COMPLETING THE UNITS

Step 1. Draw a line from corner to corner on the wrong side of all B, C, G and H squares.

Step 2. Place a B square on opposite corners of an A1 square and stitch on the marked lines as shown in Figure 2; trim seams to ¼" and press B to the right side to complete the A1-B unit, again referring to Figure 2.

Figure 2

FABRIC Measurements based on 42" usable fabric width.	#STRIPS & PIECES	CUT	#PIECES	SUBCUT
¼ yard focus fabric 1	2	6½" A1 squares with motif centered		
¼ yard focus fabric 3	5	6½" A3 squares with motif centered		
¼ yard focus fabric 4	3	6½" A4 squares		
½ yard focus fabric 2	8	6½" A2 squares with motif centered		
⅞ yard navy print	6 1	3½" x 42" 4½" x 42"	70 2	3½" C squares 4½" H squares
1¼ yards red print	6 1 6	3½" x 42" 4½" x 42" 2¼" x 42" binding	70 2	3½" B squares 4½" G squares
1¾ yards medium blue mottled	3 5	6½" x 42" 7½" x 42"	17 24 4	6½" D squares 6½" E rectangles 7½" F squares
Backing		50" x 62"		

SUPPLIES

- Batting 50" x 62"
- Neutral color all-purpose thread
- Quilting thread
- Basic sewing tools and supplies

Step 3. Repeat Step 2 with A1, A2, A3 and A4 squares and B and C to complete units as shown in Figure 3.

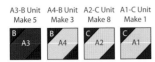

A3-B Unit Make 5 A4-B Unit Make 3 A2-C Unit Make 8 A1-C Unit Make 1

Figure 3

Step 4. Repeat Step 2 with B, C and D pieces to complete 17 D units as shown in Figure 4.

D Unit Make 17

Figure 4

Step 5. Repeat Step 2 with B and C squares with E to complete E1–E6 border units as shown in Figure 5.

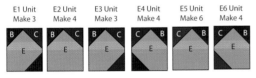

E1 Unit Make 3 E2 Unit Make 4 E3 Unit Make 3 E4 Unit Make 4 E5 Unit Make 6 E6 Unit Make 4

Figure 5

Step 6. Repeat Step 2 with B, C and F and G or H pieces to make F1 and F2 corner units as shown in Figure 6.

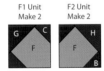

F1 Unit Make 2 F2 Unit Make 2

Figure 6

COMPLETING THE QUILT

Step 1. Arrange and join the pieced units in nine rows of seven units each referring to Figure 7; press seams in adjoining rows in opposite directions.

Step 2. Join the rows as arranged to complete the pieced top.

Step 3. Finish the quilt referring to the Finishing Instructions on page 173. ●

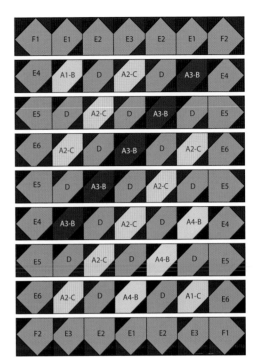

Figure 7

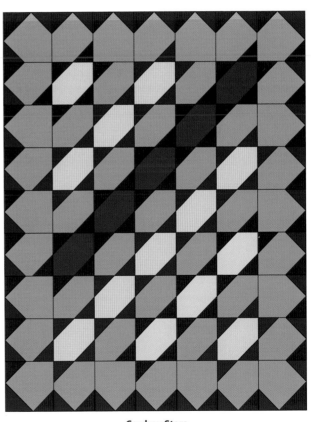

Cowboy Stars
Placement Diagram 44" x 56"

Simple Six

Design by Sue Harvey & Sandy Boobar

Six fat quarters are put to good use in this oh-so-easy quilt.

Three-Patch
10" x 10" Block
Make 6

PROJECT SPECIFICATIONS

Skill Level: Beginner
Quilt Size: 31½" x 43"
Block Size: 10" x 10"
Number of Blocks: 6

COMPLETING THE QUILT

Step 1. To complete one block, sew a C strip between two different B squares; press seams toward C.

Step 2. Sew a D strip between the B-C unit and an A rectangle referring to the block drawing for positioning; press seams toward D to complete one Three-Patch block.

Step 3. Repeat Steps 2 and 3 to make six Three-Patch blocks.

Step 4. Join two blocks with one E strip to make a row referring to the Placement Diagram for positioning; press seams toward E. Repeat to make three rows.

Step 5. Join the rows with the F strips to complete the pieced center; press seams toward F.

Step 6. Sew G strips to opposite long sides and H strips to the top and bottom of the pieced center; press seams toward G and H strips.

Step 7. Sew I strips to opposite long sides and J strips to the top and bottom of the pieced center to complete the top; press seams toward I and J strips.

Step 8. Finish the quilt referring to the Finishing Instructions on page 173. ●

FABRIC Measurements based on 42" usable fabric width.	#STRIPS & PIECES	CUT	#PIECES	SUBCUT
6 fat quarters assorted children's prints	1	5" x 10½" A from each		
	2	5" x 5" B from each		
⅔ yard novelty stripe	2	4½" x 35½" I		
	2	4½" x 32" J		
¾ yard black solid	5	1½" x 42"	2	33½" G strips
			2	24" H strips
			6	10½" D strips
			6	5" C strips
	2	2" x 42"	2	22" F strips
			3	10½" E strips
	4	2¼" x 42" binding		
Backing		38" x 49"		

SUPPLIES

- Batting 38" x 49"
- All-purpose thread to match fabrics
- Quilting thread
- Basic sewing tools and supplies

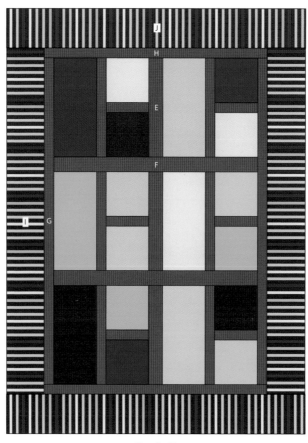

Simple Six
Placement Diagram 31½" x 43"

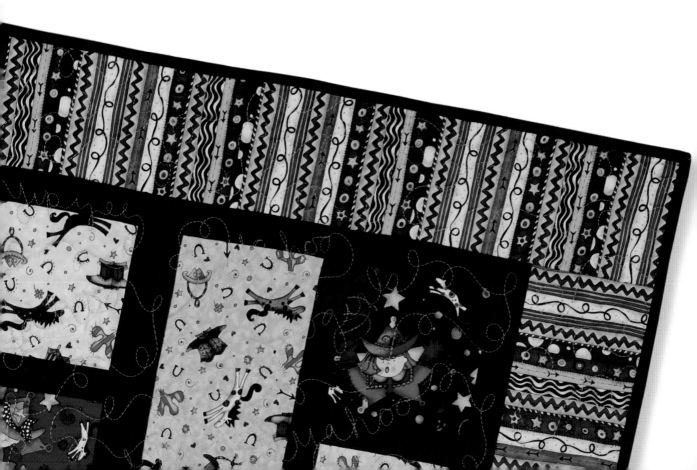

Folded Four-Patch Play Quilt

Design by Sue Harvey & Sandy Boobar

Each block in this design is a little quilt complete with backing and batting to make a cute play quilt for baby.

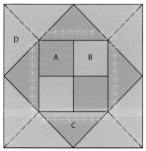

Folded Four-Patch
5³/₄" x 5³/₄" Block
Make 6 each blue, green,
pink, yellow & lavender

PROJECT SPECIFICATIONS

Skill Level: Intermediate
Quilt Size: 28¾" x 34½"
Block Size: 5¾" x 5¾"
Number of Blocks: 30

COMPLETING THE BLOCKS

Step 1. Sew a blue A strip to a B strip with right sides together along the length; press seams toward B.

Step 2. Subcut the strip set into (12) 3⅛" A-B segments as shown in Figure 1.

Figure 1   **Figure 2**

FABRIC Measurements based on 42" usable fabric width. Fabrics are batiks.	#STRIPS & PIECES	CUT	#PIECES	SUBCUT
½ yard each blue, green, yellow, pink and lavender tonals	1	3⅛" x 42" A each		
	1	3⅞" x 42" each	12	3⅞" squares; cut in half on 1 diagonal to make 24 C triangles each
2⅔ yards multicolored print	6	3⅛" x 42" B		
	8	9" x 42"	30	9" D squares

SUPPLIES

- Low-loft batting 30—5¾" squares
- Multicolored thread to match print
- Basting spray
- Basic sewing tools and supplies

Figure 3

Figure 4

Step 3. Join two A-B segments to make a Four-Patch unit as shown in Figure 2; press seam in one direction. Repeat to make six blue Four-Patch units.

Step 4. Repeat steps 1–3 to make six Four-Patch units of each color.

Step 5. To complete one blue block, place a blue C triangle right sides together on each corner of a D square. Stitch around entire square as shown in Figure 3.

Step 6. Turn triangles and seam allowance between the triangles to the wrong side of the D square as shown in Figure 4; press.

Step 7. Lightly apply basting spray to one side of a batting square. Center the square between the triangles on the D square as shown in Figure 5.

Figure 5

Figure 6

Step 8. Lightly apply basting spray to the remaining side of the batting square; center a blue Four-Patch unit on the square as shown in Figure 6.

Step 9. Fold the triangle corners over the Four-Patch unit, overlapping edges as needed as shown in Figure 7; pin in place along the outer edges of the resulting square.

Figure 7

Figure 8

Step 10. Fold each triangle corner until the point is even with, but does not extend beyond, the edge of the square as shown in Figure 8; pin in place.

Figure 9

Step 11. Using multicolored thread to match the print and a decorative stitch, machine-stitch the corner edges together and across each triangle flap as shown in Figure 9 to complete the block. *Note: Use a decorative stitch that has a centerline and extends evenly to the right and the left of the center. This is needed to stitch the corners of each block and later when the blocks are joined.*

Step 12. Repeat Steps 5–11 to complete six blue blocks and six blocks each green, pink, yellow and lavender.

COMPLETING THE QUILT

Step 1. Arrange the blocks in six rows with one block of each color in each row referring to the Placement Diagram for positioning.

Step 2. Butt the edges of two blocks from the first row. Using multicolored thread and the same decorative stitch, join the edges of the two blocks as shown in Figure 10.

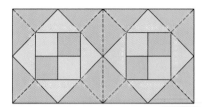
Figure 10

Step 3. Repeat Step 2 to join the blocks in each row.

Step 4. Join the rows in the same way to complete the quilt. ●

Folded Four-Patch Play Quilt
Placement Diagram 28³/₄" x 34¹/₂"

Let's Play Peekaboo

Design by Susan Knapp of The Quilt Branch

Babies love to play peekaboo and a quilt is the perfect hiding place.

PROJECT SPECIFICATIONS

Skill Level: Beginner
Quilt Size: 39" x 47"

COMPLETING THE UNITS

Step 1. Sew A to B on one short side as shown in Figure 1; press seam toward A. Repeat to make two pieced units.

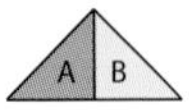

Figure 1

Step 2. Join the two pieced units as shown in Figure 2 to complete an A-B unit; press seam in one direction.

Figure 2

Step 3. Repeat Steps 1 and 2 to complete 31 A-B units.

Step 4. Draw a diagonal line from corner to corner on the wrong side of each H square.

Step 5. Place an H square right sides together on one corner of G and stitch on the marked line as shown in Figure 3; trim seam and press H to the right side, again referring to Figure 3.

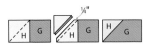

Figure 3

Step 6. Repeat Step 5 with a second H square on the remaining end of G as shown in Figure 4

FABRIC Measurements based on 42" usable fabric width.	#STRIPS & PIECES	CUT	#PIECES	SUBCUT
½ yard rainbow stripe	2	4½" x 42"	16	4½" C squares
	1	4⅞" x 42"	2	4⅞" E squares
⅝ yard yellow tonal	2	5¼" x 42"	16	5¼" squares; cut on both diagonals to make 64 B triangles
	2	2½" x 42"	20	2½" H squares
1⅛ yards rainbow print	2	4½" x 42"	12	4½" D squares
			6	2½" I rectangles
	1	2½" x 42"	8	4⅞" F/FR rectangles
	1	9⅝" x 42"	2	9⅝" squares; cut in half on 1 diagonal to make 4 L triangles
	2	3" x 34½" M		
	3	3" x 42" N		
1⅛ yards pink tonal	2	5¼" x 42"	16	5¼" squares; cut on both diagonals to make 64 A triangles
	2	2½" x 42"	10	4½" G rectangles
	5	1½" x 42"	6	18" J strips
			2	27" K strips
	5	2¼" x 42" binding		
Backing		45" x 53"		

SUPPLIES

- Batting 45" x 53"
- Neutral color all-purpose thread
- Quilting thread
- Basic sewing tools and supplies

to complete a G-H unit; repeat to complete 10 G-H units.

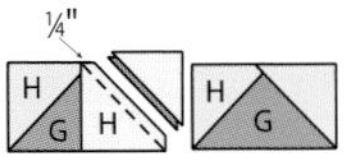

Figure 4

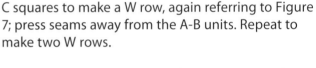

Top/bottom
Make 2

W Row
Make 2

X Row
Make 2

Y Row
Make 3

Z Row
Make 2

Figure 7

COMPLETING THE QUILT

Step 1. Measure in and mark 2½" from one end of each F/FR rectangle and cut from mark to the corner to make four each F and FR pieces as shown in Figure 5.

2½"

2½"

F   FR

Figure 5

Step 2. Cut one E square in half on one diagonal to make two E triangles as shown in Figure 6; repeat with second E square to create two reversed ER triangles, again referring to Figure 6. **Note:** *This is necessary because the square is cut from a stripe.*

E   ER

Figure 6

Step 3. Join two G-H units with F and FR and I to complete the top row as shown in Figure 7; repeat to make the bottom row. Press seams away from the G-H units.

Step 4. Join three A-B units with E and ER and two C squares to make a W row, again referring to Figure 7; press seams away from the A-B units. Repeat to make two W rows.

Step 5. Join three D squares, four A-B units and F and FR to make an X row, again referring to Figure 7; press seams away from the A-B units. Repeat to make two X rows.

Step 6. Join three A-B units with four C squares and two G-H units to complete a Y row, again referring to Figure 7; press seams toward C squares. Repeat to make three Y rows.

Step 7. Join three D squares, four A-B units and two I pieces to complete a Z row, again referring to Figure 7; press seams away from A-B units. Repeat to make two Z rows.

Step 8. Arrange and join rows as shown in Figure 8 to complete the pieced center; press seams in one direction.

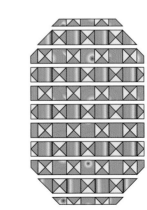

Figure 8

Step 9. Center and sew a J strip to the top and bottom of the pieced center; trim ends even with side angle using a straightedge as shown in Figure 9.

Figure 9

Step 10. Center and sew a J strip to the four angled edges and trim at each end as in Step 9.

Step 11. Center and sew a K strip to opposite long sides and trim at each end as in Step 9.

Step 12. Sew an L triangle to each corner referring to the Placement Diagram; press seams toward L.

Step 13. Sew an M strip to the top and bottom of the pieced center; press seams toward M strips.

Step 14. Join the N strips on short ends to make one long strip; press seams open. Subcut strip into two 47½" N strips.

Step 15. Sew N strips to opposite long sides of the pieced center to complete the pieced top; press seams toward M and N strips.

Step 16. Finish the quilt referring to the Finishing Instructions on page 173. ●

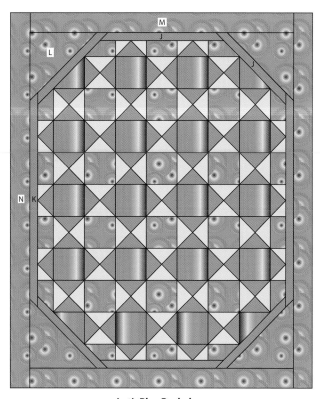

Let's Play Peekaboo
Placement Diagram 39" x 47"

Lavender Lullaby

Design by Connie Kauffman

Small, paper-pieced Log Cabin blocks in pastel colors make a perfect baby quilt.

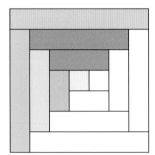

Log Cabin
3½" x 3½" Block
Make 32

PROJECT SPECIFICATIONS

Skill Level: Intermediate
Quilt Size: 28" x 35"
Block Size: 3½" x 3½"
Number of Blocks: 32

COMPLETING THE BLOCKS

Note: *Cut pieces from previously cut strips as needed for block piecing.*

Step 1. Prepare copies of paper-piecing pattern given. Set machine stitch length to 1.5 or 15 stitches to the inch.

Step 2. To complete one Log Cabin block, place piece 1 in the number 1 position on the unmarked side of the paper; pin in place. Place piece 2 right sides together with piece 1; stitch on the 1-2 line on the marked side of the paper as shown in Figure 1.

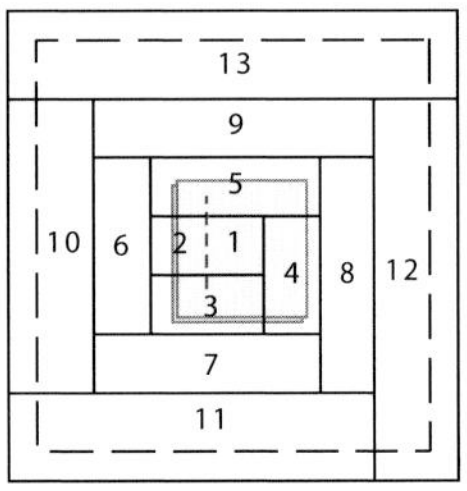

Figure 1

FABRIC Measurements based on 42" usable fabric width.	#STRIPS & PIECES	CUT	#PIECES	SUBCUT
⅛ yard each 5 pastel pink fabrics	1	1½" x 42" each fabric		
	1	2" x 21½" A each of 2 fabrics		
	1	2" x 14½" B each of 2 fabrics		
¼ yard each 5 pastel lavender fabrics	1	1½" x 42" each fabric		
	1	4" x 28½" E each of 2 fabrics		
	1	4" x 21½" F each of 2 fabrics		
¼ yard each 5 pastel green fabrics	1	1½" x 42" each fabric		
	1	2½" x 21½" C each of 2 fabrics		
	1	2½" x 14½" D each of 2 fabrics		
⅛ yard yellow tonal	2	1½" x 42"	32	1½" No. 1 squares
⅜ yard lavender mottled	4	2¼" x 42" binding		
¾ yard white tonal	14	1½" x 42"		
Backing		34" x 41"		

SUPPLIES

- Batting 34" x 41"
- Neutral color all-purpose thread
- Quilting thread
- Paper
- Basic sewing tools and supplies

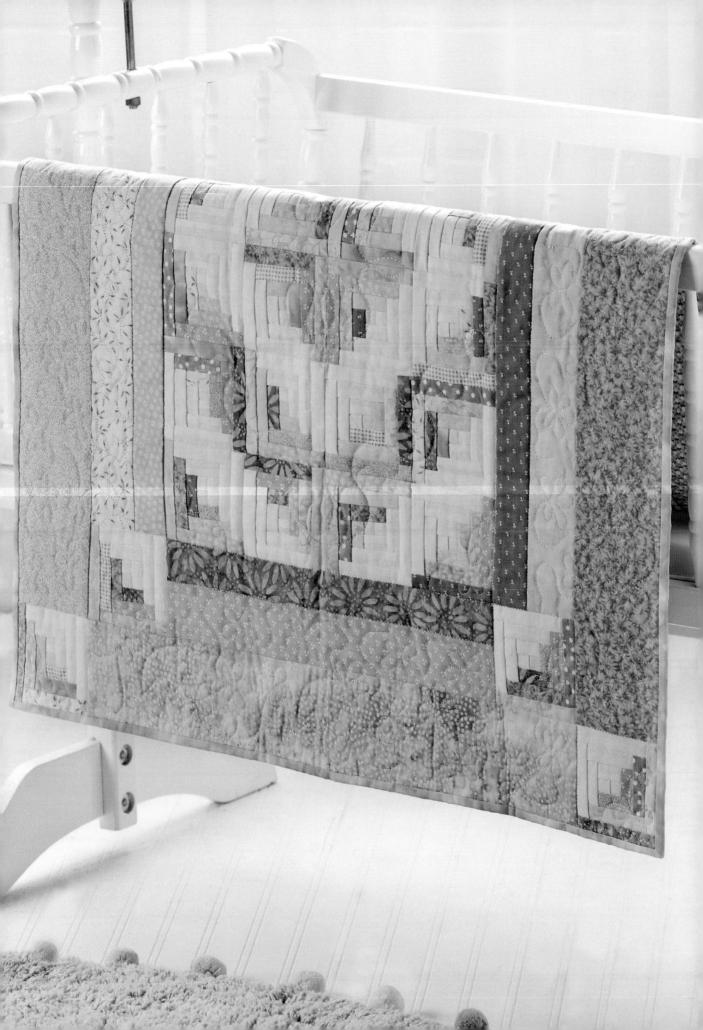

Step 3. Press piece 2 to the right side; fold back and trim the 1-2 fabric seam to ¼" if necessary and as shown in Figure 2. Repeat with pieces 3–13 in numerical order to cover the pattern.

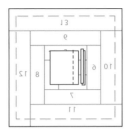

Figure 2

Step 4. Trim the pieced block unit to 4" x 4", if necessary; remove paper foundation.

Step 5. Repeat Steps 2–4 to complete 32 Log Cabin blocks.

COMPLETING THE QUILT

Step 1. Arrange and join four Log Cabin blocks to make an X row as shown in Figure 3; press seams in one direction. Repeat to make four rows.

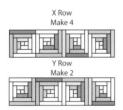

X Row
Make 4

Y Row
Make 2

Figure 3

Step 2. Join four blocks to make a Y row, again referring to Figure 3; press seams in one direction. Repeat to make two rows.

Step 3. Join the rows to complete the pieced center referring to the Placement Diagram for positioning; press seams in one direction.

Step 4. Sew an A strip to a C strip with right sides together along length; press seam toward C. Repeat to make two A-C strips.

Step 5. Repeat Step 4 with B and D strips.

Step 6. Sew an A-C strip to opposite long sides of the pieced center with the A strips toward the center; press seams toward A-C strips.

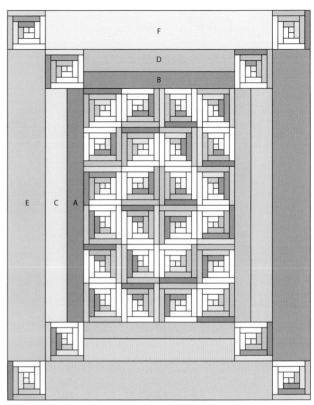

Lavender Lullaby
Placement Diagram 28" x 35"

Step 7. Sew a Log Cabin block to each end of each B-D strip as shown in Figure 4; press seams toward the B-D strips.

Figure 4

Step 8. Sew a block/B-D strip to the top and bottom of the pieced center referring to the Placement Diagram for positioning; press seams away from the pieced center.

Step 9. Sew an E strip to opposite long sides of the pieced center; press seams toward E strips.

Step 10. Sew a Log Cabin block to each end of each F strip as shown in Figure 5; press seams toward F strips.

Figure 5

Step 11. Sew the block/F strips to the top and bottom of the pieced center to complete the pieced top referring to the Placement Diagram for positioning; press seams toward the block/F strips.

Step 12. Finish the quilt referring to the Finishing Instructions on page 173. ●

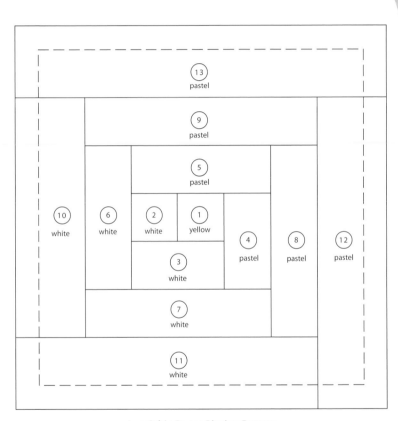

Log Cabin Paper-Piecing Pattern
Make 32 copies

Sunshine & Ribbons

Design by Ann Anderson

Showcase a special fabric, fussy-cut squares or use charm-pack squares to create the center of this quilt with a dancing ribbon border.

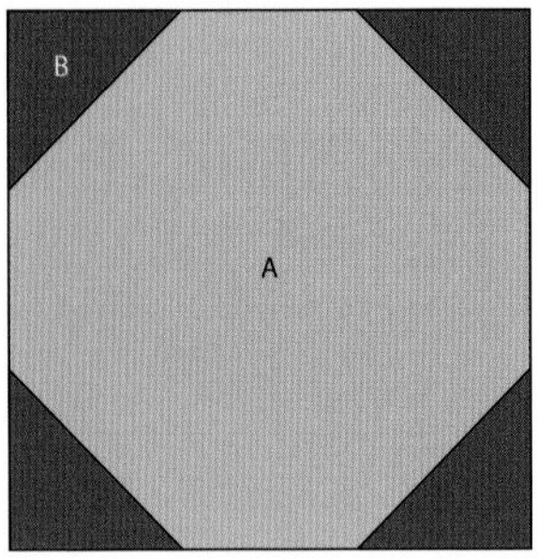

Snowball
4¼" x 4¼" Block
Make 35

PROJECT SPECIFICATIONS
Skill Level: Intermediate
Quilt Size: 44" x 52"
Block Size: 4¼" x 4¼"
Number of Blocks: 35

COMPLETING THE BLOCKS

Step 1. Mark a diagonal line from corner to corner on the wrong side of each B square.

Step 2. Place a B square right sides together on each corner of A and stitch on the marked line as shown in Figure 1; trim seam to ¼" and press seam toward B as shown in Figure 2 to complete one Snowball block. Repeat to complete 35 blocks.

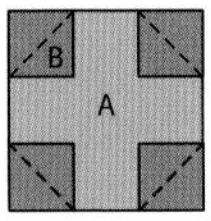

Figure 1

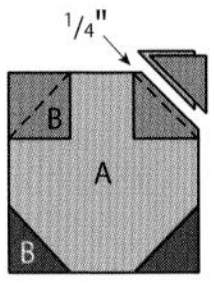

Figure 2

COMPLETING THE QUILT

Step 1. Arrange and join five blocks to make a row; press seams in one direction. Repeat to make seven rows.

Step 2. Join the rows to complete the pieced center; press seams in one direction.

FABRIC Measurements based on 42" usable fabric width.	#STRIPS & PIECES	**CUT**	#PIECES	**SUBCUT**
⅝ yard cream/ yellow print	5	2⅞" x 42"	60	2⅞" H squares
⅞ yard green/blue print or 35— 5" pre-cut charm squares	35	Fussy-cut 4¾" A squares with motif centered		
1½ yards small gold/ green/aqua floral	2	2⅜" x 33¼" E		
	2	2⅛" x 28½" F		
	3	2⅞" x 42"	40	2⅞" G squares
	1	2½" x 42"	8	2½" L squares
	3	4½" x 42"	32	2½" I rectangles
	5	2½" x 42" M/N		
1½ yards dark teal print	7	2" x 42"	140	2" B squares
	2	4½" x 42"	18	2½" K rectangles
	2	2⅞" x 42"	20	2⅞" J squares
	2	2" x 30¼" C		
	2	2" x 24¾" D		
	5	2¼" x 42" binding		
Backing		60" x 66"		

SUPPLIES

- Batting 60" x 66"
- Neutral color all-purpose thread
- Quilting thread
- Basic sewing tools and supplies

Step 3. Sew a C strip to opposite long sides and D strips to the top and bottom of the pieced center; press seams toward C and D strips.

Step 4. Sew an E strip to opposite long sides and F strips to the top and bottom of the pieced center; press seams toward E and F strips.

Step 5. Mark a diagonal line from corner to corner on the wrong side of each H square.

Step 6. Pair an H square with a G square with right sides together; stitch ¼" on each side of the marked line as shown in Figure 3.

Figure 3

Step 7. Cut the stitched unit apart on the marked line, open and press seams toward G as shown in Figure 4 to complete two G-H units. Repeat with the remaining G and H squares to complete 80 G-H units.

Make 80

Figure 4

Step 8. Repeat Steps 6 and 7 with H and J squares to complete 40 H-J units as shown in Figure 5.

Make 40

H
J

Figure 5

Step 9. Join two G-H units to make a G-H side unit as shown in Figure 6; press seam in one direction. Repeat to make 40 G-H side units.

Make 40

G
H

Figure 6

Step 10. Join five G-H side units with four I rectangles to make a side row as shown in Figure 7; press seams toward I. Repeat to make two side rows.

Figure 7

Step 11. Sew a side row to opposite sides of the pieced center with H points facing the center referring to the Placement Diagram; press seams toward E strips.

Step 12. Repeat Step 10 with four G-H side units, three I rectangles and two L squares to make the top row, starting and ending the row with an L square as shown in Figure 8; press seams toward I and L. Repeat to make the bottom row.

Figure 8

Step 13. Sew the top and bottom rows to the pieced center with H points facing the center referring to the Placement Diagram; press seams toward F strips.

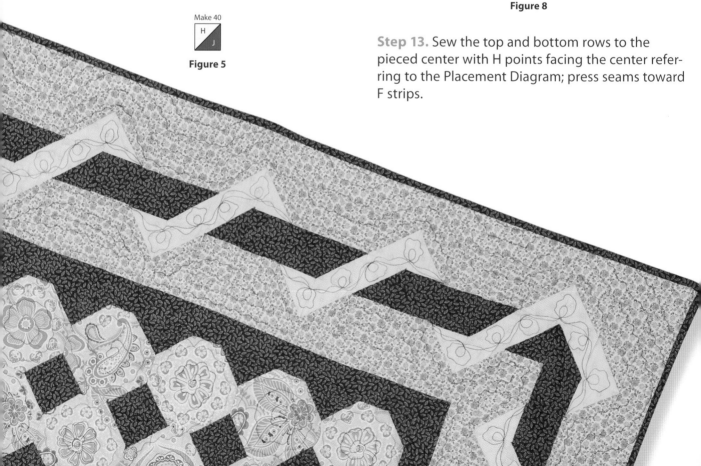

Step 14. Join two H-J units to make an H-J side unit as shown in Figure 9; press seam in one direction. Repeat to make 18 H-J side units. ***Note:*** *You will have four H-J units left for use on corners.*

Make 18

Figure 9

Step 15. Join five H-J side units with five K rectangles to make a side row as shown in Figure 10; press seams toward K. Repeat to make two side rows.

Figure 10

Step 16. Sew an H-J side row to opposite sides of the pieced center referring to the Placement Diagram for positioning of strips; press seams toward the H-J side rows.

Step 17. Join four H-J side units with two H-J units and four K rectangles to make the top row as shown in Figure 11; press seams toward K. Repeat to make the bottom row.

Figure 11

Step 18. Sew the pieced strips to the top and bottom of the pieced center; press seams toward the H-J rows.

Step 19. Join six G-H side units with five I rectangles to make a long G-H side row as shown in Step 12; press seams toward I. Repeat to make two long G-H side rows and sew to opposite long sides of the pieced center referring to the Placement Diagram for positioning; press seams toward the long G-H side rows.

Figure 12

Step 20. Repeat Step 19 with five G-H side units, four I rectangles and two L squares as shown in Figure 13; press seams toward I and L. Repeat to make the bottom row.

Figure 13

Step 21. Sew the top and bottom rows to the pieced center referring to the Placement Diagram for positioning of rows; press seams away from the pieced center.

Step 22. Join the M/N strips on short ends to make one long strip; press seams open. Subcut strip into two 48½" M strips and two 44½" N strips.

Step 23. Sew M strips to opposite long sides and N strips to the top and bottom of the pieced center to complete the pieced top; press seams toward the M and N strips.

Step 24. Finish the quilt referring to the Finishing Instructions on page 173. ●

Sunshine & Ribbons
Placement Diagram 44" x 52"

Pooches & Patches

Design by Nancy Richoux

A simple Nine-Patch block combines with an appliquéd dog design in this pastel-colored baby quilt.

PROJECT SPECIFICATIONS
Skill Level: Beginner
Quilt Size: 35" x 35"
Block Size: 9" x 9"
Number of Blocks: 9

Pooch
9" x 9" Block
Make 5

Nine-Patch
9" x 9" Block
Make 4

COMPLETING THE NINE-PATCH BLOCKS

Step 1. Sew a B square between two A squares to make an A-B-A row as shown in Figure 1; press seams toward A. Repeat to make two A-B-A rows.

Figure 1

Step 2. Sew an A square between two B squares to make a B-A-B row as shown in Figure 2; press seams toward A.

Figure 2

FABRIC Measurements based on 42" usable fabric width.	#STRIPS & PIECES	CUT	#PIECES	SUBCUT
Scraps white solid and black print		Appliqué pieces as per pattern		
¼ yard light blue print		Appliqué pieces as per pattern		
¼ yard medium blue print		Appliqué pieces as per pattern		
½ yard pink print	2	3½" x 42" Appliqué piece as per pattern	16	3½" B squares
½ yard light green print	2	3½" x 42"	20	3½" A squares
⅔ yard white print	2	9½" x 42"	5	9½" C squares
1⅞ yards pastel-colored stripe	8	2½" x 42"	6	9½" D
			4	2½" x 31½" E
			2	2½" x 35½" F
	1	41" x 41" backing		

SUPPLIES

- Batting 41" x 41"
- Neutral color all-purpose thread
- Quilting thread
- Black fine-point permanent fabric marker
- Basic sewing tools and supplies

Step 3. Sew the B-A-B row between the two A-B-A rows to complete one Nine-Patch block referring to the block drawing; press seams in one direction.

Step 4. Repeat Steps 1–3 to complete four Nine-Patch blocks.

COMPLETING THE QUILT

Step 1. Join two Pooch blocks with green collars with one Nine-Patch block and two D strips to make an X row; press seams toward D strips. Repeat to complete two X rows.

Step 2. Join two Nine-Patch blocks with the Pooch block with pink collar and two D strips to make a Y row; press seams toward D strips.

Step 3. Join the X and Y rows with two E strips to complete the pieced center; press seams toward E strips.

Step 4. Sew an E strip to opposite sides and F strips to the top and bottom of the pieced center to complete the pieced top; press seams toward E and F strips.

Step 5. Finish the quilt referring to the Finishing Instructions on page 173, trimming batting even with the pieced top and trimming backing ¾" larger all around. Turn under the backing edge ¼", bring backing to the front and hand-stitch in place to finish. ●

COMPLETING THE POOCH BLOCKS

Step 1. Prepare templates for each appliqué piece using pattern given; trace shapes onto the right side of fabrics using a fine lead pencil. Cut out pieces, adding a ¼" seam allowance all around.

Step 2. Turn under seam allowance on each piece along the marked line; baste to hold in place.

Step 3. Fold and crease each C square to mark the vertical and horizontal centers.

Step 4. Using full-size pattern as a guide, center a pooch motif on a C square and hand-appliqué in place in numerical order; remove basting.

Step 5. Use the black fine-point permanent fabric marker to mark mouth, whisker dots and eyebrows.

Step 6. Repeat Steps 4 and 5 to complete five Pooch blocks.

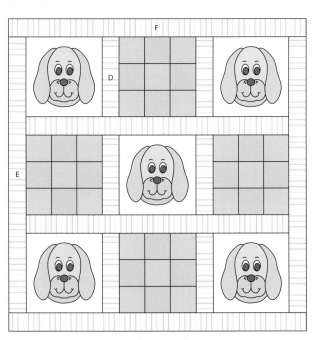

Pooches & Patches
Placement Diagram 35" x 35"

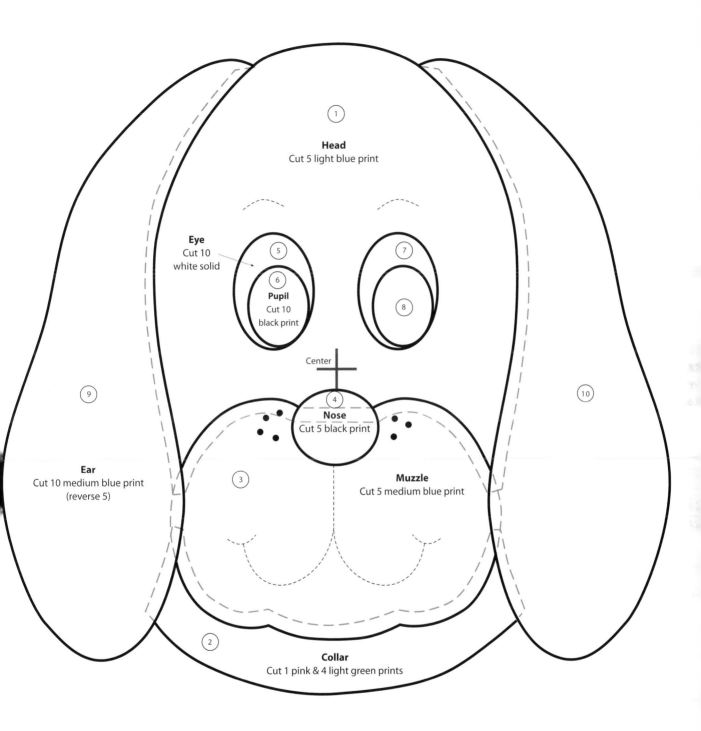

Head
Cut 5 light blue print

Eye
Cut 10
white solid

Pupil
Cut 10
black print

Center

Nose
Cut 5 black print

Ear
Cut 10 medium blue print
(reverse 5)

Muzzle
Cut 5 medium blue print

Collar
Cut 1 pink & 4 light green prints

Spring Bright Baby Quilt

Design by Christine Schultz

Frame a focus fabric with bright strips and attract Baby's attention.

● ●

PROJECT SPECIFICATIONS

Skill Level: Beginner
Quilt Size: 38" x 45"
Block Size: 7" x 7"
Number of Blocks: 20

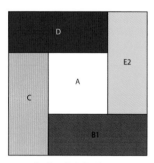

Spring Bright B1-E2
7" x 7" Block
Make 4

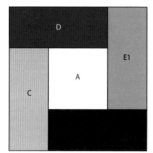

Spring Bright B2-E1
7" x 7" Block
Make 6

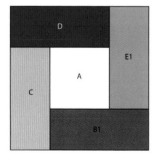

Spring Bright B1-E1
7" x 7" Block
Make 4

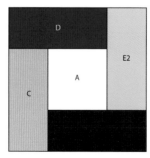

Spring Bright B2-E2
7" x 7" Block
Make 6

FABRIC Measurements based on 42" usable fabric width.	#STRIPS & PIECES	CUT	#PIECES	SUBCUT
1 fat quarter each orange tonal (E1) and yellow/orange print (E2)	10	2½" x 5½" E1 rectangles		
	13	2½" x 5½" E2 rectangles		
1 fat quarter each 2 red tonals (B1 and B2)	10	2½" x 5½" B1 rectangles		
	13	2½" x 5½" B2 rectangles		
1 fat quarter light green tonal	3	5½" x 21"	23	2½" C rectangles
1 fat quarter dark green print	3	5½" x 21"	23	2½" D rectangles
1½ yards white print	2	3½" x 42"	20	3½" A squares
	1	5½" x 42"	8	3½" F rectangles
	2	5½" x 28½" G strips		
	2	5½" x 21½" H strips		
	5	2¼" x 42" binding		
Backing		44" x 51"		

SUPPLIES

- Batting 44" x 51"
- Neutral color all-purpose thread
- Quilting thread
- Basic sewing tools and supplies

Figure 1

Figure 2

COMPLETING THE BLOCKS

Step 1. Stitch B2 to A, stopping stitching 1" from the end of A to make a partial seam as shown in Figure 1; press seam toward B.

Step 2. Add C, D and then E1 to the sides of A as shown in Figure 2; press seams away from A.

Step 3. Complete the B-E seam as shown in Figure 3 to complete one Spring Bright B2-E1 block; press seam toward B.

Figure 3

Step 4. Repeat Steps 1–4 to complete six blocks each with B2-E1 and B2-E2 and four blocks each with B1-E1 and B1-E2 .

COMPLETING THE QUILT

Step 1. Join two each B2-E1 and B2-E2 Spring Bright blocks to make an X row as shown in Figure 4; press seams in one direction. Repeat to make three X rows.

Step 2. Repeat Step 1 with two each B1-E1 and B1-E2 Spring Bright blocks to make a Y row, again referring to Figure 4; press seams in the opposite direction of the X rows. Repeat to make two Y rows.

X Row
Make 3

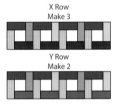

Y Row
Make 2

Figure 4

Step 3. Join the rows to complete the pieced center referring to the Placement Diagram for positioning; press seams in one direction.

Step 4. Sew E2 to F to make an E2-F unit as shown in Figure 5; press seam away from F. Repeat to make two E2-F units.

Figure 5

Step 5. Sew B1 to F and add C to complete a B1-C-F unit as shown in Figure 6; press seams toward B1 and then C.

Figure 6

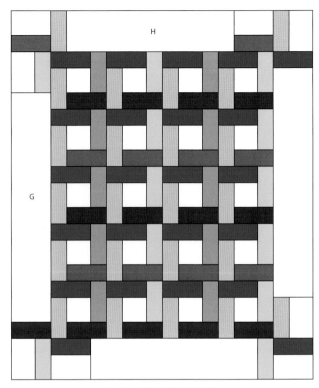

Spring Bright Baby Quilt
Placement Diagram 38" x 45"

Step 6. Sew C to F to complete a C-F unit as shown in Figure 7; press seams toward C. Repeat to make two C-F units.

Figure 7

Step 7. Sew D to F and add E2 to make a D-E2-F unit as shown in Figure 8; press seams toward D and E2.

Figure 8

Step 8. Sew D to F to make a D-F unit as shown in Figure 9; press seam toward D.

Figure 9

Step 9. Sew an E2-F unit to one end and a B2 rectangle to the opposite end of one G strip to complete the G1 strip as shown in Figure 10; press seam toward G.

Figure 10

Step 10. Sew the G1 strip to the right side edge of the pieced center referring to the Placement Diagram for positioning; press seam toward the G strip.

Step 11. Sew D to one end and a C-F unit to the opposite end of the remaining G strip to complete the G2 strip, again referring to Figure 10; press seams away from G.

Step 12. Sew the G2 strip to the left side edge of the pieced center referring to the Placement Diagram for positioning; press seam toward the G strip.

Step 13. Sew the B1-C-F, B1-C and C-F units to H as shown in Figure 11 to make the H1 strip; press seams toward H.

Figure 11

Step 14. Sew the H1 strip to the top of the pieced center referring to the Placement Diagram for positioning; press seams toward the H strip.

Step 15. Sew the E2-F unit, the two D-F units and an E2 rectangle to the remaining H strip as shown in Figure 12 to make the H2 strip; press seams toward H.

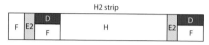

Figure 12

Step 16. Sew the H2 strip to the bottom of the pieced center to complete the pieced top referring to the Placement Diagram for positioning; press seams toward the pieced H strip.

Step 17. Finish the quilt referring to the Finishing Instructions on page 173. ●

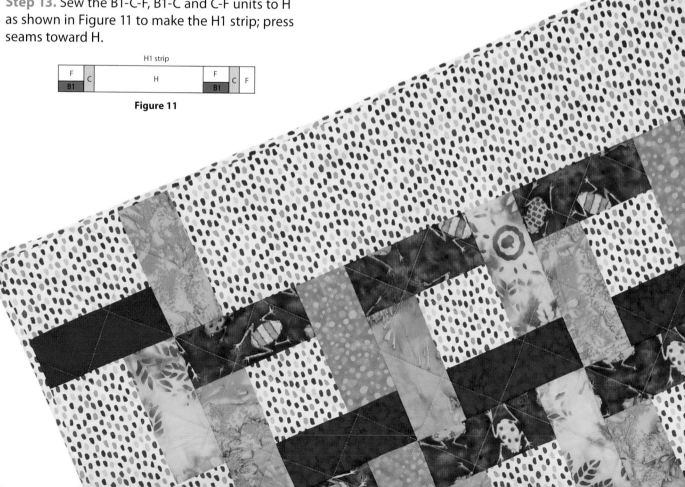

Just Ducky Baby Quilt

Design by Mary Kerr

A duck pull-toy is duplicated in a fun and colorful baby quilt.

Just Ducky
9¹/₂" x 11" Block
Make 9

PROJECT SPECIFICATIONS

Skill Level: Beginner
Quilt Size: 42½" x 47"
Block Size: 9½" x 11"
Number of Blocks: 9

COMPLETING THE BLOCKS

Step 1. Trace appliqué shapes onto the paper side of the fusible web as directed on patterns for number to cut; cut out shapes, leaving a margin around each one.

Step 2. Fuse shapes to the wrong side of fabrics as directed on patterns for color; cut out shapes on traced lines. Remove paper backing.

Step 3. Fold and crease each A rectangle to mark the vertical and horizontal centers.

Step 4. Center and fuse a duck motif on each A rectangle, fusing pieces in numerical order.

FABRIC Measurements based on 42" usable fabric width.	#STRIPS & PIECES	CUT	#PIECES	SUBCUT
Scraps black solid and brown tonal		Appliqué pieces as per pattern		
Scraps red, blue, orange 1, orange 2 and pink tonals		Appliqué pieces as per patterns		
⅜ yard purple tonal	2	4" x 42" Appliqué pieces as per pattern	16	4" C squares
⅜ yard each yellow/ orange prints 1 and 2		Appliqué pieces as per patterns		
⅝ yard royal blue check	5	3" x 42" binding		
⅔ yard aqua tonal	2	10" x 42"	12	4" D rectangles
¾ yard green print	2	11½" x 42"	12	4" B rectangles
1¼ yards white confetti print	3	11½" x 42"	9	10" A rectangles
Backing		48" x 53"		

SUPPLIES

- Batting 48" x 53"
- All-purpose thread to match fabrics and black
- Quilting thread
- 1¼ yards 18"-wide fusible web
- 1¼ yards fabric stabilizer
- Water-erasable marker or pencil
- Basic sewing tools and supplies

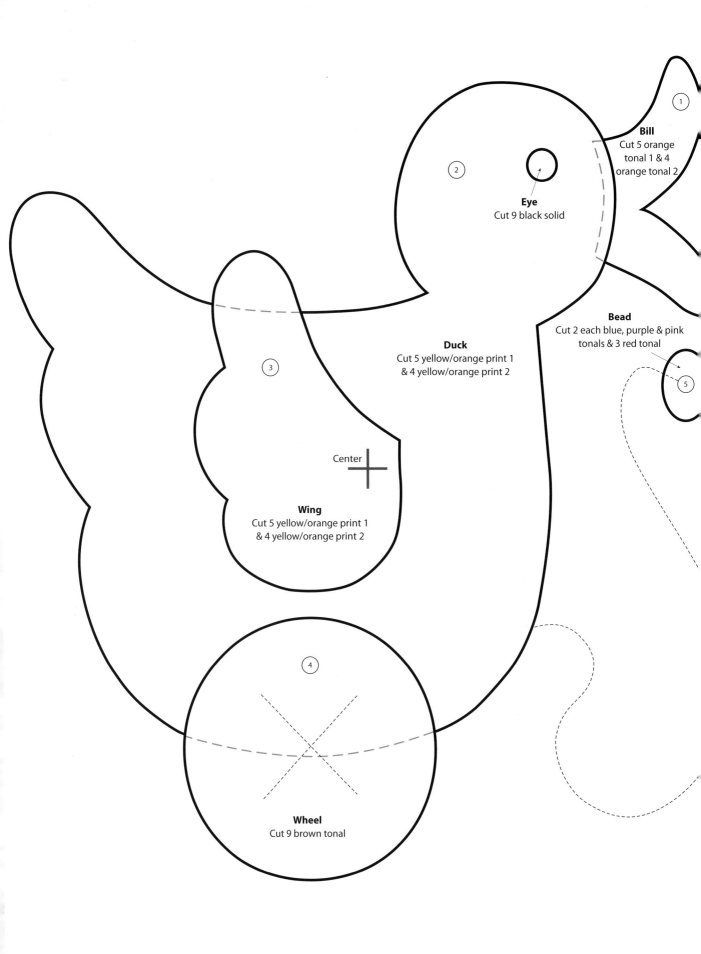

①

Bill
Cut 5 orange
tonal 1 & 4
orange tonal 2

②

Eye
Cut 9 black solid

Bead
Cut 2 each blue, purple & pink
tonals & 3 red tonal

③

⑤

Duck
Cut 5 yellow/orange print 1
& 4 yellow/orange print 2

Center

Wing
Cut 5 yellow/orange print 1
& 4 yellow/orange print 2

④

Wheel
Cut 9 brown tonal

Step 5. Transfer wheel and pull string placement on the fused blocks using the full-size pattern and a water-erasable marker or pencil.

Step 6. Cut nine 9" x 10" rectangles fabric stabilizer; pin to the wrong side of each fused block.

Step 7. Satin-stitch around all duck shapes using orange thread and all beads using matching thread; blanket-stitch around the wheel shapes and satin-stitch X inside wheels using brown thread.

Step 8. Satin-stitch along the marked string lines and around eye shapes using black thread.

Step 9. Remove fabric stabilizer to complete nine Just Ducky blocks.

COMPLETING THE QUILT
Step 1. Join three Just Ducky blocks with four B rectangles to complete a block row; press seams toward B. Repeat to make three block rows.

Step 2. Join three D rectangles with four C squares to make a sashing row; press seams toward D. Repeat to make four sashing rows.

Step 3. Join the block rows with the sashing rows to complete the pieced top; press seams toward sashing rows.

Step 4. Finish the quilt referring to the Finishing Instructions on page 173. ***Note:*** *Use a ½" seam allowance to stitch binding to quilt edge.* ●

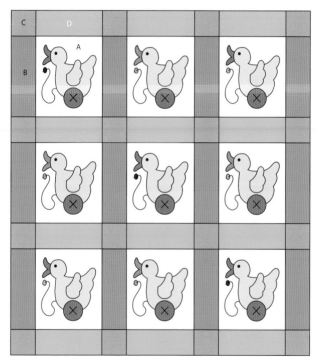

Just Ducky Baby Quilt
Placement Diagram 42½" x 47"

Crazy-Patch Safari

Design by BrendaBarb Designs/Brenda Connelly and Barb Miller

Appliquéd motifs on a crazy-patchwork background make a fun baby quilt.

PROJECT SPECIFICATIONS

Skill Level: Intermediate
Quilt Size: 33" x 40½"
Block Size: 7½" x 7½"
Number of Blocks: 12

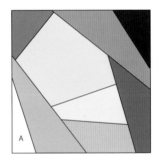

Crazy-Patch A
7½" x 7½" Block
Make 9

Crazy-Patch B
7½" x 7½" Block
Make 3

COMPLETING THE BLOCKS

Step 1. Prepare a template for piece A using pattern given on page 56; cut as directed.

Step 2. Trace template A on one corner of nine muslin foundation squares as shown in Figure 1.

Figure 1

Figure 2

Step 3. Center a scrap on one muslin square for piece 1; place a second scrap right sides together with piece 1 and stitch along one side as shown in Figure 2. Press piece 2 to the right side.

FABRIC Measurements based on 42" usable fabric width.	#STRIPS & PIECES	CUT	#PIECES	SUBCUT
Scraps bright-colored children's prints, mottleds and tonals		For crazy-patch pieces		
Scraps red, yellow, purple and orange		Appliqué pieces as per patterns		
⅜ yard white mottled		A pieces as per template Random pieces for crazy patchwork Appliqué pieces as per patterns		
⅜ yard black solid	5	2" x 42"	1	35" E strip
			3	24½" D strips
			1	2" K square
			2	15½" C pieces
			1	33½" H strip
¾ yard lime green mottled	4	3½" x 42"	1	3½" x 35" F strip
			1	33½" I strip
			1	5" J piece
			1	2" L piece
			1	33½" G strip
			1	29" M strip
	4	2¼" x 42" binding		
⅞ yard muslin	3	8" x 42"	12	8" foundation squares
Backing		39" x 46"		

SUPPLIES

- Batting 39" x 46"
- All-purpose thread to match fabrics
- Quilting thread
- Machine-embroidery threads as desired
- ½ yard 12"-wide fusible web
- Black, red and various other colors permanent fabric pens
- Fabric glue
- Basic sewing tools and supplies and index card

Step 4. Continue adding pieces around the center piece until the square is covered.

Step 5. Find the marked corner and trim the fabric piece covering the marked area to ¼" beyond the inside marked line as shown in Figure 3.

Figure 3

Step 6. Pin A right sides together with the trimmed piece and stitch; press A to the right side.

Step 7. Trim stitched unit to 8" x 8", leaving the A corner untrimmed to complete one Crazy-Patch A block.

Step 8. Repeat Steps 3–7 to complete nine Crazy-Patch A blocks.

Step 9. Complete three Crazy-Patch B blocks as for Crazy-Patch A blocks except without adding A to the corner.

Step 10. Use decorative threads and your sewing machine's fancy stitches to embellish along seam lines and as desired on all blocks.

ADDING APPLIQUE TO CRAZY-PATCH BLOCKS

Step 1. Trace appliqué shapes given onto the paper side of the fusible web; cut out shapes, leaving a margin around each one.

Step 2. Fuse shapes to the wrong side of scraps as directed on each piece; cut out shapes on traced lines. Remove paper backing.

Step 3. Fuse a circle onto one B block center, then fuse the giraffe shape on top, referring to the Placement Diagram for positioning.

Step 4. Fuse the elephant shape onto one B block, cutting legs to copy the angle on a piece in the block, making it appear that the legs are behind the piece.

Step 5. Fuse a second circle to the center of an A block; center and fuse the heart shape on top.

Step 6. Cut the face and ear shapes away from the lion mane. Arrange and fuse the body shape and then the mane on top on a B block. *Note: The body color will show through to make the face and ears of the lion.*

Step 7. Using the permanent fabric pens, add details to each fused shape as marked on patterns.

Step 8. Using black thread and a machine buttonhole stitch, stitch around the lion body, elephant and giraffe shapes. Straight-stitch around lion's head, white circles and heart shapes using thread to match fabrics.

COMPLETING THE QUILT

Step 1. Arrange and join two Crazy-Patch A blocks to make a row as shown in Figure 4; press seam in one direction. Repeat to make two rows.

Step 2. Join the rows to make an A section, again referring to Figure 4; repeat to make two A sections. Press seams in one direction.

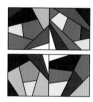

Figure 4

Step 3. Join two B blocks to make a vertical B row as shown in Figure 5; press seam in one direction.

Step 4. Join one A and one B block to make a vertical A/B row as shown in Figure 6; press seam in one direction.

Figure 5 **Figure 6**

Step 5. Join the vertical B row with one A section and one C strip as shown in Figure 7 to complete the top section. Press seams toward C.

Step 6. Repeat Step 4 with the vertical A/B row and the remaining A section to complete the bottom section as shown in Figure 8.

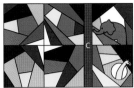

Figure 7

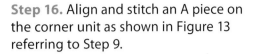

Figure 8

Step 7. Join the top and bottom sections with D and sew a second D to the top to complete the pieced center; press seams toward D.

Step 8. Fold the diagonal seam allowance of A over the edge of an index card and press to make creased seam as shown in Figure 9; remove index card and secure seam with fabric glue to hold. Repeat with two more A pieces.

Step 9. Place an A piece on a D strip with the side and bottom edges of A aligned with the edges of D as shown in Figure 10; machine-baste A to outer edge of D.

Figure 9

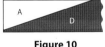

Figure 10

Step 10. Machine buttonhole-stitch A in place along the diagonal seam using white thread.

Step 11. Sew the A-D strip to the bottom of the pieced center referring to the Placement Diagram for positioning; press seam toward A-D.

Step 12. Sew E and then F to the right-side edge of the pieced center and M to the bottom; press seam toward E, F and M.

Step 13. Sew the H strip to the I strip with right sides together along the length; press seam toward the H strip.

Step 14. Align and stitch an A piece on the bottom corner to complete the A/H-I strip as shown in Figure 11 referring to Step 9.

Figure 11

Step 15. Sew K to L; press seam toward K. Add J to complete the corner unit referring to Figure 12; press seam toward J.

Figure 12

Step 16. Align and stitch an A piece on the corner unit as shown in Figure 13 referring to Step 9.

Figure 13

Step 17. Sew the A/corner unit to the A/H-I strip as shown in Figure 14; press seam toward the A/H-I strip.

Step 18. Sew the pieced strip to the left-side edge of the pieced center; press seam toward the pieced strip.

Step 19. Sew the G strip to the top to complete the pieced top; press seams toward G strip.

Step 20. Finish the quilt referring to the Finishing Instructions on page 173. ●

Figure 14

Crazy-Patch Safari
Placement Diagram 33" x 40½"

A
Cut 12 white mottled

Giraffe
Cut 1 yellow scrap

Elephant
Cut 1 purple scrap

Lion Body
Cut 1 yellow scrap

Lion Mane
Cut 1 orange scrap

Circle
Cut 2 white mottled

Heart
Cut 1 red scrap

Fun Baby Accessories

Babies are so adorable that anything you quilt for them will bring joy to baby and mother alike; quilting for baby is irresistible.

Discovery Baby Quilt

Design by Connie Rand

Little ones will love finding the ladybugs and frogs under the flaps and putting fun stuff in the pockets of this quilt.

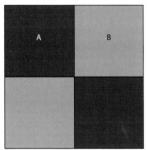

Four-Patch
7" x 7" Block
Make 18

PROJECT SPECIFICATIONS

Skill Level: Beginner
Quilt Size: 45" x 59"
Block Size: 7" x 7"
Number of Blocks: 18

COMPLETING THE BLOCKS

Step 1. Sew an A strip to a B strip with right sides together along the length to make an A-B strip set; press seams toward B. Repeat to make four A-B strip sets.

Step 2. Subcut the A-B strip sets into (36) 4" A-B units as shown in Figure 1.

Figure 1

Step 3. Join two A-B units to make a Four-Patch block; press seams in one direction. Repeat to make 18 Four-Patch blocks.

COMPLETING THE QUILT

Step 1. To make pockets, place C and D squares right sides together and join along upper edge as shown in Figure 2. Flip so the wrong sides are together; press and topstitch ¼" from finished edge, again referring to Figure 2. Repeat to make four pockets.

FABRIC FOR QUILT Measurements based on 42" usable fabric width.	#STRIPS & PIECES	CUT	#PIECES	SUBCUT
4 assorted motif 7½" G squares				
1 fat quarter yellow print	4	7½" C squares		
1 fat quarter multicolored check	4	7½" F squares		
⅝ yard red print	4	4" x 42" A		
⅝ yard orange print	4	4" x 42" B		
⅝ yard green print	2	7½" x 42"	9	7½" E squares
¾ yard blue print	3	7½" x 42"	12	7½" D squares
1½ yards coordinating lengthwise stripe	2	5½" x 49½" H along length		
	2	5½" x 45½" I along length		
Backing		51" x 65"		

SUPPLIES

- Batting 51" x 65"
- Neutral color all-purpose thread
- Quilting thread
- Basic sewing tools and supplies

Figure 2

Step 2. Place each pocket piece on a D square as shown in Figure 3. Baste sides and lower edge to complete pockets.

Figure 3

Step 3. Place F and D squares right sides together and stitch on three sides. Turn right side out, press and topstitch as shown in Figure 4 to make flaps.

Figure 4

Step 4. Join Four-Patch blocks with pockets, and E and G squares as shown in Figure 5 to make X, Y and Z rows. Pin flaps to G squares at top edges, again referring to Figure 5.

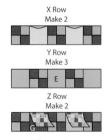

Figure 5

Step 5. Join rows to complete quilt center referring to the Placement Diagram, being careful not to catch the pocket top openings or the flap bottom edges in the seams between rows.

Step 6. Sew H strips to opposite sides and I strips to the top and bottom of the pieced center to complete the pieced top; press seams toward H and I strips.

Step 7. Finish the quilt referring to the Finishing Instructions on page 173. ●

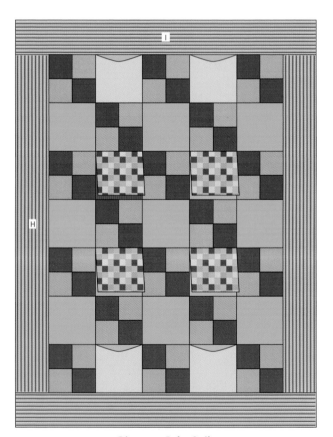

Discovery Baby Quilt
Placement Diagram 45" x 59"

I Spy Four-Patch

Design by Sandra L. Hatch

Make scrappy strips using all those leftover children's scraps you've accumulated over time.

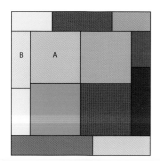

Framed Four-Patch
11" x 11" Block
Make 12

PROJECT SPECIFICATIONS

Skill Level: Beginner
Quilt Size: 46" x 57"
Block Size: 11" x 11"
Number of Blocks: 12

COMPLETING THE BLOCKS

Step 1. Select four A squares; join in two sets of two squares each. Press seams in opposite directions.

Step 2. Join the two A sets to complete the block center as shown in Figure 1; press seam in one direction. Repeat to make 12 A units.

Figure 1

Step 3. Join the 2"-wide scrap strips on short ends to make one 700"-long B strip; press seams open.

Step 4. Lay the B strip right sides together on an A unit and stitch as shown in Figure 2. Continue adding all A units to the strip.
***Note:** If you don't like how a seam appears when sewing A units to the strip, skip to another area on the strip as desired.*

Figure 2

FABRIC FOR QUILT	#STRIPS & PIECES	CUT
Measurements based on 42" usable fabric width. Fabrics are flannel.		
48—4½" scrap squares children's prints for A		
Variety of 2"-wide scrap B strips to equal 700"		
Variety of 2¼"-wide scrap strips to equal 210" for binding		
1 yard orange mottled	2	2½" x 37½" D
	3	2½" x 42" C
	5	3½" x 42" G/H
Backing		52" x 63"

SUPPLIES

- Batting 52" x 63"
- Neutral color all-purpose thread
- Quilting thread
- Basic sewing tools and supplies

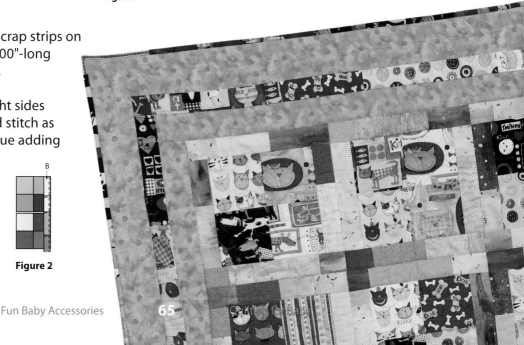

Step 5. Lay the stitched A-B units on a flat surface and cut close to edge of A units using a straight-edge and a rotary cutter as shown in Figure 3; press seams toward the B strips.

Figure 3

Step 6. Continue Steps 4 and 5 first on the opposite side of the A units, and then the top and bottom to complete 12 blocks; press seams away from the A units after trimming each time.

COMPLETING THE QUILT

Step 1. Join three blocks to make a row; press seams in one direction. Repeat to make four rows.

Step 2. Join the rows, alternating row pressing as needed, to complete the pieced center.

Step 3. Join C strips on short ends to make one long strip; press seams open. Subcut strip into two 44½" C strips.

Step 4. Sew a C strip to opposite long sides and D strips to the top and bottom of the pieced center; press seams toward C and D strips.

Step 5. Cut two 48½" E strips and two 40½" F strips from the B scrap strip.

Step 6. Sew an E strip to opposite long sides and F strips to the top and bottom of the pieced center; press seams toward E and F strips.

Step 7. Join G/H strips on short ends to make one long strip; press seams open. Subcut strip into two 51½" G strips and two 46½" H strips.

Step 8. Sew a G strip to opposite long sides and H strips to the top and bottom of the pieced center; press seams toward G and H strips.

Step 9. Finish the quilt referring to the Finishing Instructions on page 173. ●

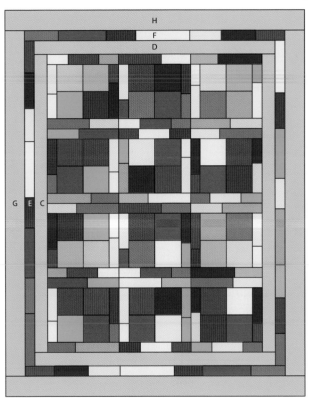

I Spy Four-Patch
Placement Diagram 46" x 57"

Little Lamb Bib & Burp Pad

Designs by Mary Ayres

Jelly roll strips of large and small dotted pastel colors using large and small dotted fabrics make this cute baby bib and burp pad.

PROJECT SPECIFICATIONS

Skill Level: Beginner
Bib Size: 8" x 8"
Burp Pad Size: 8" x 20"

COMPLETING THE BURP PAD

Step 1. Join the A strips along length to make an 8½" x 30" A unit; press seams in one direction.

Step 2. Cut off an 8½" length and set side for bib; trim remaining A unit to a 20½" length.

Step 3. Using the bib pattern corner, round the corners of the long A unit as shown in Figure 1.

Figure 1

Step 4. Trace lamb pieces onto the paper side of the fusible web referring to pattern for number to cut; cut out shapes, leaving a margin around each one.

Step 5. Fuse shapes to the wrong side of fabrics as directed on patterns for color to cut; cut out shapes on traced lines. Remove paper backing. Set aside reverse lamb body and one lamb head for bib.

Step 6. Center and fuse lamb shapes 1" from one end of the A unit referring to the Placement Diagram for positioning.

FABRIC Measurements based on 42" usable fabric width.	#STRIPS & PIECES	CUT
Scraps white tonal and yellow dot		Appliqué pieces as per pattern
⅛ yard each pink, lavender, blue and green dots	1	2½" x 30" A each fabric
⅓ yard white terry cloth	1	9" x 22" burp pad backing
	1	9" x 9" bib backing

SUPPLIES

- Batting 9" x 22", 9" x 9"
- Neutral color all-purpose thread
- Quilting thread
- ¼ yard fusible web
- Pink and white embroidery floss
- 4 yards pink small rickrack
- Basic sewing tools and supplies

Step 7. Using 2 strands pink embroidery floss, blanket-stitch around the edges of each piece.

Step 8. Using 3 strands of pink embroidery floss, straight-stitch eyes and short nose lines.

Step 9. Stem-stitch long nose lines and bow using 1 strand of pink embroidery floss.

Step 10. Baste rickrack around the right-side edges of the A unit with center of rickrack ¼" from cut edge as shown in Figure 2.

¼"

Figure 2

Step 3. Embroider as in Steps 7–9 for Burp Pad.

Step 4. Baste rickrack in place around side and bottom edges.

Step 5. Layer appliquéd top with the terry cloth backing and batting, and stitch all around, leaving a 3" opening on one straight edge.

Step 6. Trim batting close to seam; turn right side out. Turn opening edges in ¼"; hand-stitch in place. Press edges flat.

Step 7. Cut a 35" length of rickrack; center at bib center and pin in place across top curved edge, leaving ends extended for bib ties.

Figure 3

Step 8. Using 6 strands white embroidery floss, blanket-stitch rickrack in place, placing the inside line of each stitch in the center of each dip of the rickrack as shown in Figure 3 to finish. ●

Step 11. Place the appliquéd A unit right side together on top of the white terry cloth backing piece; place batting on the bottom. Trim batting and backing to the same size as the A unit.

Step 12. Stitch all around edge, leaving a 4" opening on one long side; trim batting close to seam. Turn right side out through opening.

Step 13. Turn opening edges in ¼" and hand-stitch opening closed. Press edges flat to finish.

COMPLETING THE BIB

Step 1. Using bib pattern given, cut bib shape from the 8½" square previously cut from the stitched A unit; cut backing and batting as directed.

Step 2. Center the reversed lamb motif 1" from bottom edge and fuse in place.

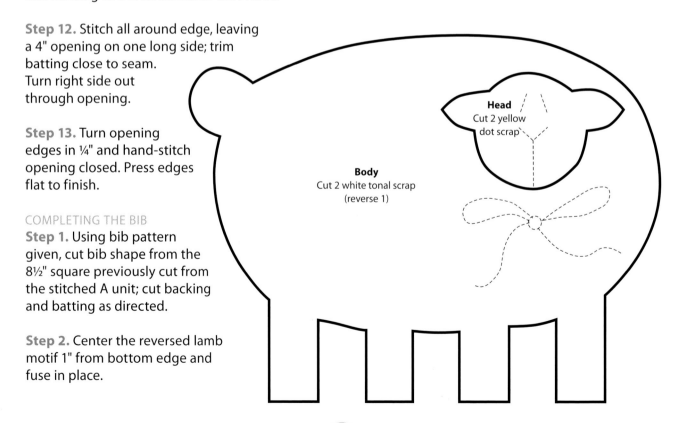

Head
Cut 2 yellow
dot scrap

Body
Cut 2 white tonal scrap
(reverse 1)

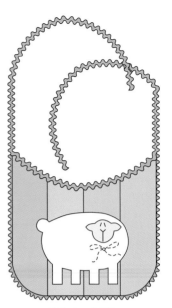

Little Lamb Bib
Placement Diagram 8" x 8"

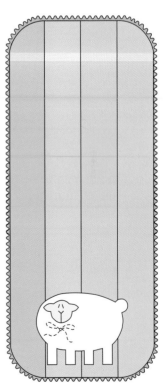

Little Lamb Burp Cloth
Placement Diagram 8" x 20"

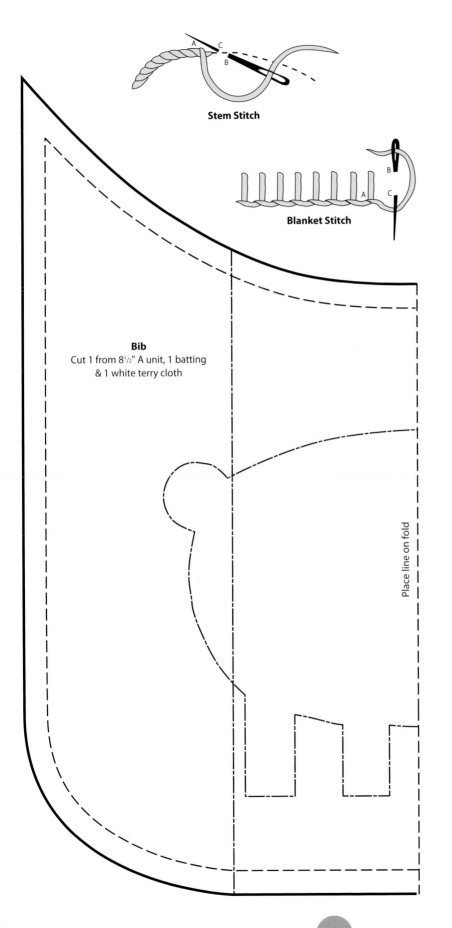

Stem Stitch

Blanket Stitch

Bib
Cut 1 from 8½" A unit, 1 batting
& 1 white terry cloth

Place line on fold

Whirligigs Changing Mat

Design by Julie Weaver

Roll up this handy mat and tuck it into your diaper bag.

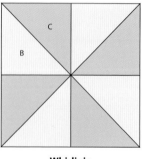

Whirligig
4" x 4" Block
Make 20

PROJECT SPECIFICATIONS

Skill Level: Beginner
Quilt Size: 22" x 30"
Block Size: 4" x 4"
Number of Blocks: 20

COMPLETING THE WHIRLIGIG BLOCKS

Step 1. Draw a diagonal line from corner to corner on the wrong side of each B square.

Step 2. Pair a B square with a C square with right sides together; stitch ¼" on each side of the marked line as shown in Figure 1.

Figure 1

Figure 2

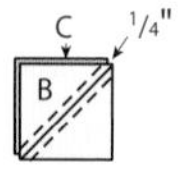

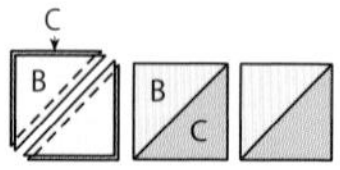

Step 3. Cut apart on the marked line to complete two B-C units as shown in Figure 2; press seams toward C.

Step 4. Repeat Steps 2 and 3 to complete 80 B-C units.

Step 5. To complete one Pinwheel block, join two B-C units to make a row; repeat. Press seams in one direction.

FABRIC Measurements based on 42" usable fabric width.	#STRIPS & PIECES	CUT	#PIECES	SUBCUT
⅜ yard cream print	3	2⅞" x 42"	40	2⅞" B squares
⅜ yard green print	3	2⅞" x 42"	40	2⅞" C squares
⅞ yard green mottled	1	12½" x 20½" A		
	2	1½" x 28½" D		
	2	1½" x 22½" E		
	3	2½" x 42" binding		
Backing		28" x 36"		

SUPPLIES

• Batting 28" x 36"
• Neutral color all-purpose thread
• Quilting thread
• Basic sewing tools and supplies

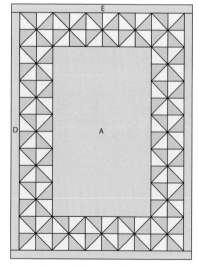

Whirligigs Changing Mat
Placement Diagram 22" x 30"

Step 6. Join the two rows referring to the block drawing to complete one block; press seam in one direction.

Step 7. Repeat Steps 5 and 6 to make 20 blocks.

COMPLETING THE MAT
Step 1. Join five Pinwheel blocks to make a row as shown in Figure 3; press seams in one direction. Repeat to make four rows.

Step 2. Sew a row to opposite sides and to the top and bottom of A to complete the pieced center; press seams toward A.

Step 3. Sew D strips to opposite long sides and E strips to the short ends of the pieced center to complete the pieced top; press seams toward D and E strips.

Step 4. Finish the mat referring to the Finishing Instructions on page 173. ●

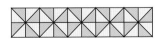

Figure 3

Denim All-Boy Tote

Design by Chris Malone

Make a denim bag for a special baby boy.

⬤ ⬤

PROJECT SPECIFICATIONS
Skill Level: Intermediate
Bag Size: 14" x 12" x 4"

COMPLETING THE BAG
Note: *All seams are ¼" with right sides together unless otherwise instructed. A walking foot is very helpful when sewing through the layers of denim and fleece.*

Step 1. Bond the matching-size fusible fleece pieces to the wrong side of the tote front, back and gusset pieces, working from the center of each piece to the outside.

Step 2. To make an outside pocket, join a denim pocket piece to the pocket lining along one 14½" edge; press seam open. Flip the lining over so the wrong sides are together. Repeat with remaining outside pocket and lining.

Step 3. Fold the sewn edge of one pocket down 2" so the lining shows; pin to tote front, matching side and bottom edges. Repeat with second pocket and tote back; machine-baste ³⁄₁₆" from raw edges as shown in Figure 1.

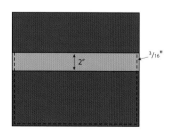

Figure 1

FABRIC FOR QUILT Measurements based on 42" usable fabric width except as noted.	#STRIPS & PIECES	CUT
Scraps 4 coordinating prints	16	2½" x 2½" A squares
	4	3" diameter circles for button covers
⅝ yard green print	2	14½" x 12½" front and back linings
	1	4½" x 38½" inside gusset strip
	4	2½" x 2½" A squares
⅝ yard blue stripe	2	14½" x 10½" lining for outside pockets
	4	8½" x 5½" for inside pockets
	4	2½" x 2½" A squares
¾ yard 54"-wide blue denim	2	14½" x 12½" front and back pieces
	1	4½" x 39½" outside gusset strip
	2	14½" x 10½" outside pockets
	2	3½" x 24½" B
⅝ yard 45"-wide fusible fleece	2	14½" x 12½"
	1	4½" x 39½"

SUPPLIES

- All-purpose thread to match fabric
- 4 (1½") buttons to cover
- 3¾" x 13¾" strip heavyweight cardboard or plastic needlepoint canvas
- Basic sewing tools and supplies, chalk marker and optional walking foot

Step 4. Measure 4⅞" from each side on the tote front pocket only and mark a chalk line; lift pocket flat and stitch on marked line up to fold line to divide pocket as shown in Figure 2.

Figure 2

Step 5. Follow manufacturer's directions to cover the buttons with fabric.

Step 6. Sew two buttons to each side of the tote on the pocket flap as shown in Figure 3.

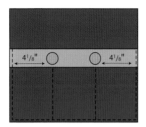

Figure 3

Step 7. To make the patchwork handle, sew 12 A squares together to make an A strip; press seams in one direction. Repeat to make two A strips.

Step 8. With right sides together, sew one long side of B to one long side of the A strip; press seams toward the A strip. Repeat with the remaining long edge. ***Note:*** *The B strip is wider than the A strip.* Repeat to make two A-B strips.

Step 9. Turn the A-B strips right side out; press so the denim B strip forms a ¼" border down the long sides of each strip as shown in Figure 4; topstitch along seam line between the A and B strips, again referring to Figure 4.

Figure 4

Step 10. Pin the ends of one A-B strip to the right side of the tote front 2¾" from the side seams and matching short ends of the strip to the top edge of the tote as shown in Figure 5. ***Note:*** *The denim/B side of the strip should be facing out.* Stitch in place; repeat to add the second strip to the tote back to complete handle application.

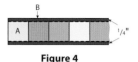

Figure 5

Step 11. Sew one long edge of the outside gusset to the sides and bottom of the tote front; stitch down one side and stop ¼" from the bottom with the needle down. Pivot the tote and reposition the gusset along the edge. Stitch to the next corner and repeat the pivot; trim the gusset end even with the tote front as necessary referring to Figure 6.

Figure 6

Step 12. To make pockets for lining, pin two 8½" x 5½" inside pockets right sides together and sew all around, leaving a 2" opening along one side. Clip the corners and turn right side out. Fold in the seam allowance on the opening and press; repeat for second inside pocket.

Step 13. Center one pocket 3" down from the top edge on the right side of a lining rectangle; sew to lining by stitching close to the edge on both sides and along the bottom as shown in Figure 7. ***Note:*** *If desired, divide the pocket by stitching down the center of the pocket.* Repeat with the second pocket and remaining lining piece.

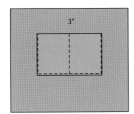

3"

Figure 7

Step 14. Prepare the lining in the same manner as for the tote, Step 11, by sewing the inside gusset between the lining front and back; press side seams open. Do not turn right side out.

Step 15. Fold under a ¼" hem at the upper edge of the lining and press.

Step 16. Place the cardboard or plastic strip in the bottom of the tote.

Step 17. Insert the lining into the tote shell, matching side seams.

Step 18. Fold the tote handles up and fold the top edge in ¼"; slipstitch the folded edge of the lining to the folded edge of the tote.

Step 19. Topstitch all around the top edge of the tote ³⁄₁₆" from edge to finish. ●

Denim All-Boy Tote
Placement Diagram 14" x 12" x 4"

Peekaboo Monkeys

Design by Connie Kauffman

Monkeys play peekaboo with Baby on this appliquéd play quilt.

• •

PROJECT SPECIFICATIONS
Skill Level: Beginner
Quilt Size: 33" x 37"

PREPARING THE APPLIQUÉ
Step 1. Trace appliqué shapes onto the paper side of the fusible web as directed on patterns; cut out shapes, leaving a margin around each one.

Step 2. Fuse shapes to the wrong side of fabrics as directed on patterns for color to cut; cut out shapes on traced lines. Remove paper backing.

Step 3. Transfer face details to patterns using a water-erasable marker or pencil.

Step 4. Using the appliqué pressing sheet, layer the monkey-head motifs and fuse pieces in place using patterns as guides under the sheet.

COMPLETING THE QUILT
Step 1. Lay out the A strips referring to the Placement Diagram for positioning.

Step 2. Arrange and fuse the single monkey tails and the No. 4 paws, and the Monkey 2 head and ear 2A motif on the A strips referring to the Placement Diagram for approximate positioning of pieces.

Step 3. Join A strips with right sides together along length referring to the Placement Diagram for placement; press seams in one direction.

Step 4. Sew a B strip to a C strip; press seam toward B strip. Repeat to make two B-C strips.

Step 5. Sew a B-C strip to opposite long sides of the pieced center; press seams toward B-C strips.

Step 6. Sew a D strip to the top and bottom of the pieced center; press seams toward D strips.

FABRIC Measurements based on 42" usable fabric width.	#STRIPS & PIECES	CUT
Scrap black solid		Appliqué pieces as per patterns
⅛ yard tan solid		Appliqué pieces as per patterns
⅛ yard white tonal		Appliqué pieces as per patterns
¼ yard brown tonal		Appliqué pieces as per patterns
¼ yard each 6 green prints	1	4½" x 28½" A each
	2	4½" x 3½" E each
⅓ yard dark brown print	2	1½" x 28½" B
	4	1½" x 3½" F
	2	1½" x 33" D
⅓ yard green leaf print	2	4" x 28½" C
	4	4" x 3½" G
Backing		39" x 43"

SUPPLIES
- Batting 39" x 43"
- All-purpose thread to match fabrics
- Quilting thread
- Black embroidery floss
- 1 yard 12"-wide fusible web
- ⅝ yard fabric stabilizer
- Appliqué pressing sheet
- Water-erasable marker or pencil
- Basic sewing tools and supplies

Step 7. Arrange and join two each F and G pieces with six E rectangles as shown in Figure 1 and the Placement Diagram; press seams toward F. Repeat to make two E-F-G strips.

Figure 1

Step 8. Sew an E-F-G strip to the top and bottom of the pieced center.

Step 9. Arrange and fuse the remaining monkey-head motifs and pieces on the quilt top referring to the Placement Diagram for positioning.

Step 10. Cut pieces of fabric stabilizer to fit behind each fused shape; pin in place.

Step 11. Using a machine blanket stitch and thread to match fabrics, machine-appliqué all fused shapes in place; remove fabric stabilizer.

Step 12. Straight-stitch mouth, nose, eyelashes and eyebrows using 1 strand of black embroidery floss to complete the top.

Step 13. Complete the quilt referring to the Finishing Instructions on page 173. ●

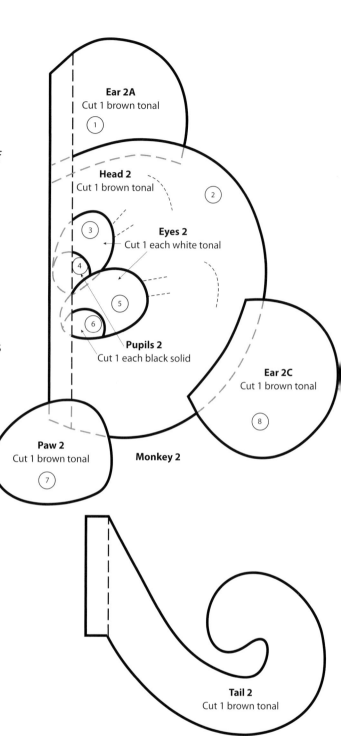

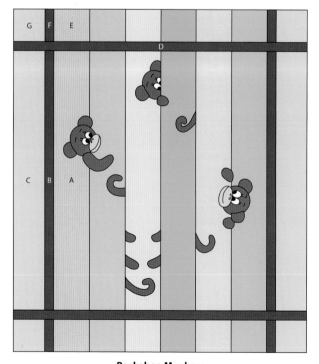

Peekaboo Monkeys
Placement Diagram 33" x 37"

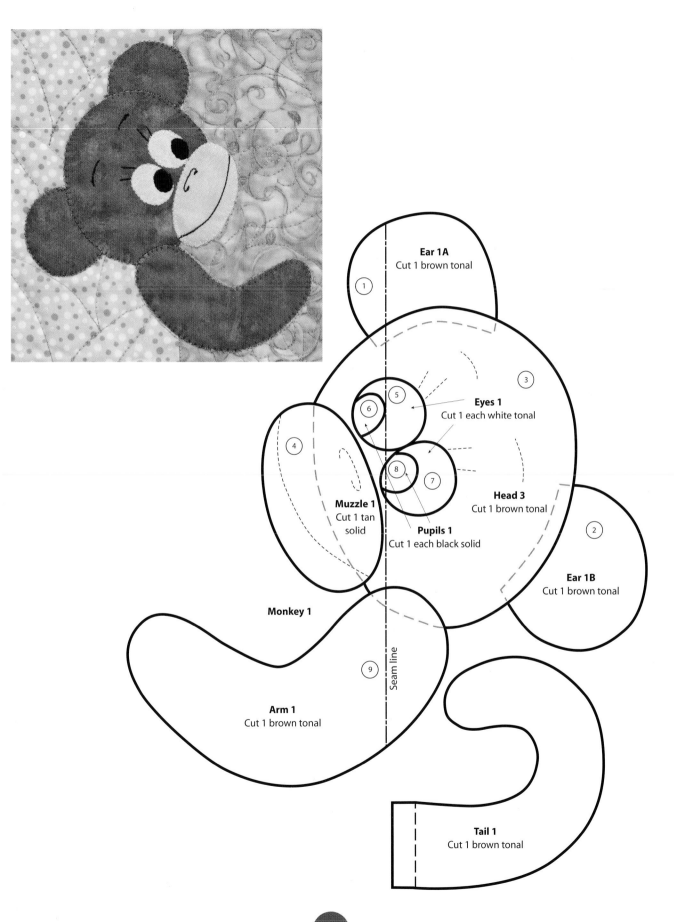

Ear 1A
Cut 1 brown tonal

1

3

5

6

Eyes 1
Cut 1 each white tonal

4

8

7

Muzzle 1
Cut 1 tan
solid

Head 3
Cut 1 brown tonal

2

Pupils 1
Cut 1 each black solid

Ear 1B
Cut 1 brown tonal

Monkey 1

9

Seam line

Arm 1
Cut 1 brown tonal

Tail 1
Cut 1 brown tonal

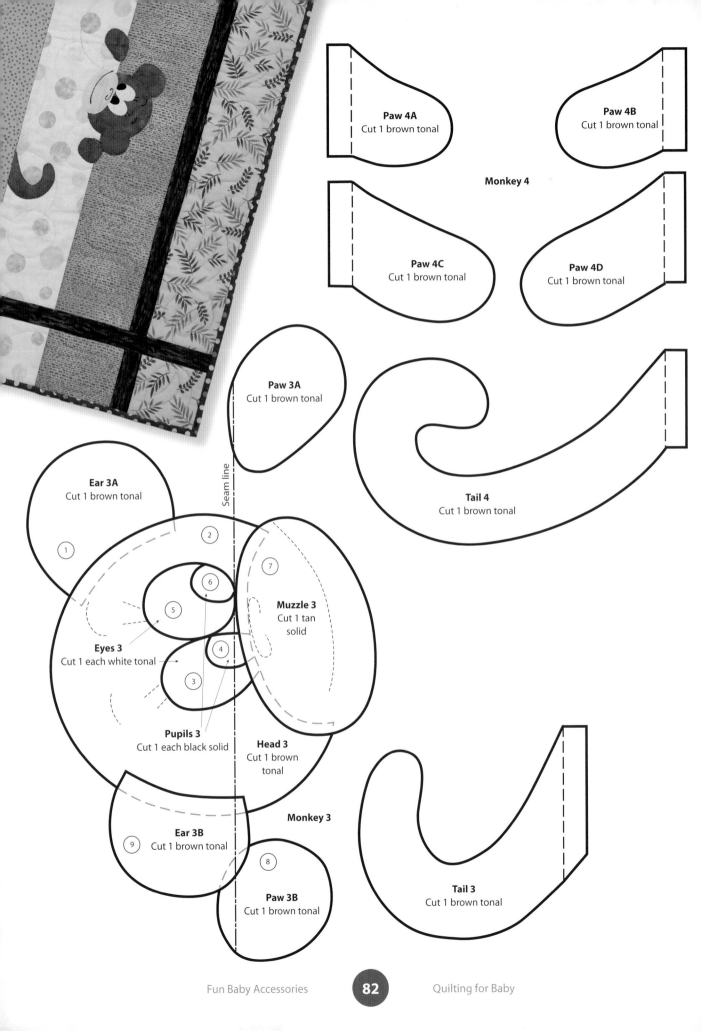

Paw 4A
Cut 1 brown tonal

Paw 4B
Cut 1 brown tonal

Monkey 4

Paw 4C
Cut 1 brown tonal

Paw 4D
Cut 1 brown tonal

Paw 3A
Cut 1 brown tonal

Tail 4
Cut 1 brown tonal

Ear 3A
Cut 1 brown tonal

Seam line

Muzzle 3
Cut 1 tan
solid

Eyes 3
Cut 1 each white tonal

Pupils 3
Cut 1 each black solid

Head 3
Cut 1 brown
tonal

Monkey 3

Ear 3B
Cut 1 brown tonal

Paw 3B
Cut 1 brown tonal

Tail 3
Cut 1 brown tonal

Cute as a Button

Design by Chris Malone

*Buttons adorn this cute wall hanging focused
on a baby photo in the center.*

PROJECT SPECIFICATIONS
Skill Level: Intermediate
Hanging Size: 15" x 11" without ribbons

PROJECT NOTE
Choose fabric colors to coordinate with the colors
in your photo, especially noting the clothing
and background.

COMPLETING THE HANGING
Step 1. Scan or download your photo into your
computer and resize as needed to make a 4½" x 4½"
square for the center. Print first on paper to check
size and placement. Follow manufacturer's instructions for printing on the fabric sheet, and for drying
and setting the print.

Step 2. Trim the completed print to 4½" x 4½";
set aside.

Step 3. Transfer the "cute as a" phrase to the center
of one B square referring to the pattern and using
an air-erasable pen referring to Figure 1. ***Note:***
*Remember when centering phrase that a button
is stitched at the end of the phrase and should be
included when centering.*

Figure 1

FABRIC FOR QUILT Measurements based on 42" usable fabric width.	#STRIPS & PIECES	CUT
4 assorted print scraps	2	2" x 4½" A
	2	2½" x 7½" C
	2	2½" x 7½" D
	4	2½" x 2½" G
		See instructions for cutting flowers
Scrap green tonal		See instructions for cutting leaves
Fat quarter white tonal	2	8" x 8" B
⅛ yard red tonal	1	1½" x 42" E
⅛ yard yellow print	1	1½" x 42" F
Backing		15½" x 11½"

SUPPLIES

- Batting 15½" x 11½"
- Neutral color all-purpose thread
- Quilting thread
- Embroidery floss to match flower fabric
- 6 (18") lengths assorted coordinating satin ribbons, ⅝"–1¼" wide
- 1 (1⅛") novelty flower button
- 22 (½"–¾") assorted white buttons
- 2 (½") white shank buttons
- Permanent fabric glue
- Scrap lightweight nonwoven interfacing
- 2 (¾") plastic rings
- Computer and color printer
- Sheet of white computer-printable fabric and color photo
- Basic sewing tools and supplies, air-erasable pen and 6" embroidery hoop

Step 4. Using 2 strands of matching embroidery floss, backstitch over the marked lines, using French knots for dots.

Step 5. Use alphabet pattern given to center and transfer the baby's name to the remaining B piece. *Note: Enlarge letters given for uppercase. Change embroidery floss color to match photo, if desired.*

Step 6. Press embroidered B pieces; trim to 7½" x 2" with lettering (and button area) centered.

Step 7. Sew A strips to opposite sides of the photo square and B strips to the top and bottom as shown in Figure 2; press seams toward A and B strips.

Figure 2

Step 8. Sew C to D; press seam toward D. Repeat to make two C-D units.

Step 9. Sew a C-D unit to the A sides of the pieced unit as shown in Figure 3; press seams toward C-D units.

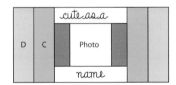

Figure 3

Step 10. Sew the E strip to the F strip with right sides together along length; press seam toward E strip.

Step 11. Subcut the E-F strip set into (22) 1½" E-F units as shown in Figure 4.

Figure 4

Step 12. Join 11 E-F units to make an E-F strip as shown in Figure 5; press seams in one direction. Repeat to make two E-F strips.

Figure 5

Step 13. Sew a G square to each end of each E-F strip; press seams toward G.

Step 14. Sew a G/E-F strip to the top and bottom of the pieced center referring to the Placement Diagram for positioning; press seams toward the pieced center.

Step 15. Cut the ribbons in half and arrange randomly along the bottom edge, starting ⅜" from each corner; when satisfied with arrangement, pin each ribbon end to the pieced center and machine-baste in place as shown in Figure 6.

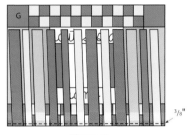

Figure 6

Step 16. Place the batting on a flat surface with the pieced top right side up on top; pin the backing piece right sides together with the pieced top.

Step 17. Sew all around, leaving a 4" opening along one side. Clip corners; trim batting close to the stitching.

Step 18. Turn right side out through opening; press, folding the seam allowance inside at the opening. Slipstitch the opening closed.

Step 19. Hand- or machine-quilt in the ditch of the border seams and an echo square in the G pieces to complete basic construction.

ADDING BUTTONS & FLOWERS

Step 1. Trace two large flower shapes on the wrong side of a fabric scrap. Fold the fabric in half with right sides together with the marked shapes on top; pin to the interfacing.

Step 2. Sew all around on the marked lines; cut out ⅛" from the stitching line as shown in Figure 7.

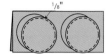

Figure 7

Step 3. Cut a slash through one layer only; turn each flower right side out through the slash; whip-stitch the slashed openings closed. Repeat to make two small flowers using a contrasting scrap.

Step 4. Layer one small flower on one larger flower with slashed sides down; sew a shank button to the center, sewing through all layers.

Step 5. Using thread to match the top flower, sew a small (about ⅝") circle of gathering stitches around the center on the back of the large flower; pull the thread to gather the flower around the button center. Knot thread and then sew flower to a top corner G square. Repeat with second set of flowers for remaining top corner G square.

Step 6. Trace the leaf pattern six times on the wrong side of the green tonal. Fold the fabric in half with right sides together and pattern on top; pin to interfacing. Sew on marked lines, leaving open at straight edge of each leaf.

Step 7. Cut out ⅛" from stitching; trim interfacing close to seam. Clip curves and turn right side out.

Step 8. Fold in raw edges ³⁄₁₆" at bottom open edge; slipstitch to hold.

Step 9. Fold and tack a small pleat in the center of each leaf base as shown in Figure 8.

Figure 8

Step 10. Arrange three leaves around each flower; tack or glue base of each leaf in place.

Step 11. Sew the novelty button to the end of the saying on the top B strip.

Step 12. Sew a white button to the E squares in the E-F strips referring to the Placement Diagram.

Step 13. Trim the ribbon ends to make equal length; fold each end in half along length and cut at an angle to form a V as shown in Figure 9.

Figure 9

Step 14. Whipstitch a plastic ring on the top back corners of the wall quilt for hanging. ●

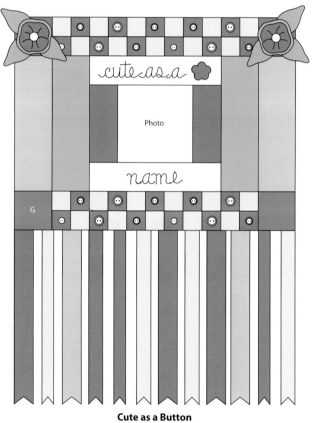

Cute as a Button
Placement Diagram 15" x 11" (without ribbons)

Phrase

Tip

For a quicker version, enlarge a computer font and print the saying and name on another sheet of printable fabric.

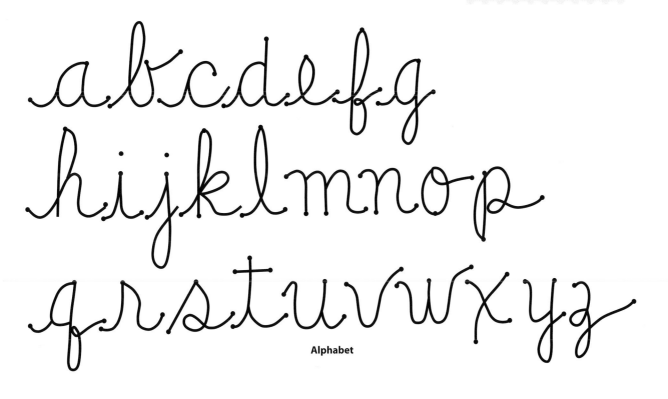

Alphabet

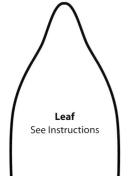

Leaf
See Instructions

Large Flower
See Instructions

Small Flower
See Instructions

Fun Frog Play Mat

Design by Sue Harvey & Sandy Boobar

There are lots of fun things to keep Baby busy at this frog pond!

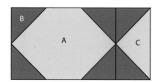

Fish
8" x 4" Block
Make 4 each color

PROJECT SPECIFICATIONS
Skill Level: Beginner
Quilt Size: 52" x 52"
Block Size: 8" x 4"
Number of Blocks: 16

COMPLETING THE BLOCKS

Step 1. Mark a line from corner to corner on the wrong side of each B square.

Step 2. Place B right sides together on opposite corners of A as shown in Figure 1; stitch on the marked line, trim seam allowance to ¼" and press B to the right side, again referring to Figure 1. Repeat on the remaining corners of A to complete one A-B unit, again referring to Figure 1. Repeat with all A rectangles to complete four A-B units of each color.

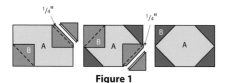

Figure 1

Step 3. Repeat Step 2 with B squares and C rectangles to complete four B-C units of each color as shown in Figure 2.

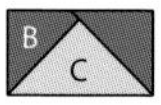

Figure 2

Step 4. Sew an A-B unit to a same-color B-C unit to complete one Fish block referring to the block

drawing for positioning; press seam toward A-B. Repeat to complete four blocks of each color.

FABRIC Measurements based on 42" usable fabric width.	#STRIPS & PIECES	CUT	#PIECES	SUBCUT
Scraps white and black fleece		Appliqué pieces as per pattern		
¼ yard each yellow and salmon fleece		Pieces as per patterns		
¼ yard each red, orange and yellow prints and tonals	1	4½" x 42" each	4	6½" A rectangles each
			4	2½" C rectangles each
½ yard green fleece		Pieces as per patterns		
⅔ yard lime green print	1	4½" x 42"	4	6½" A rectangles
			4	2½" C rectangles
	6	2¼" x 42" binding		
1 yard green/ blue stripe	4	6½" x 40½" H Frog piece as per pattern		
1⅔ yards blue water print	6	2½" x 42"	96	2½" B squares
	2	4½" x 42"	16	4½" D squares
	1	8½" x 42"	1	8½" E square
			2	16½" F rectangles
	2	8½" x 32½" G		
	1	6½" x 42"	4	6½" I squares
Backing		58" x 58"		

SUPPLIES
- Batting 58" x 58" and 10" x 20"
- All-purpose thread to match fabrics
- Quilting thread
- Polyester fiberfill
- 4 toy squeakers
- 1 toy shaker
- Fabric glue
- 1 toy ring (optional)
- Basic sewing tools and supplies

COMPLETING THE TOP

Step 1. Sew a different-color Fish block to opposite sides of E as shown in Figure 3; press seams toward E.

Step 2. Sew D to each end of the two remaining color Fish blocks, facing the fish in opposite directions as shown in Figure 3; press seams toward D. Sew the pieced strips to the remaining sides of E, again referring to Figure 3; press seams toward the strips.

Figure 3

Step 3. Sew F to two opposite sides and G to the remaining sides of the pieced unit; press seams toward F and G.

Step 4. Join three Fish blocks with two D squares to complete a side strip as shown in Figure 4; press seams toward D. Repeat to make four strips.

Figure 4

Step 5. Sew a strip to opposite sides of the pieced center referring to the Placement Diagram for positioning of strips; press seams toward the pieced center.

Step 6. Sew D to each end of the remaining strips; press seams toward D. Sew a strip to the remaining sides of pieced center; press seams toward the pieced center.

Step 7. Sew H to opposite sides of the pieced center; press seams toward H.

Step 8. Sew I to each end of the remaining H strips; press seams toward I. Sew the strips to the remaining sides to complete the top; press seams toward the H-I strips.

COMPLETING THE QUILT

Step 1. Sandwich the batting between the completed top and prepared backing; pin, baste or spray-baste to hold.

Step 2. Quilt as desired; remove pins or basting, if necessary. Trim batting and backing even with the quilted top.

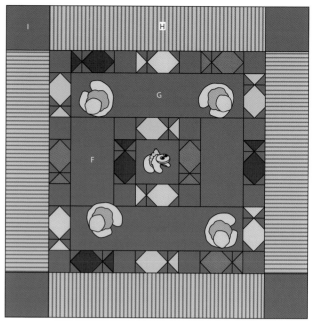

Fun Frog Play Mat
Placement Diagram 52" x 52"

Step 3. Join the binding strips on short ends with diagonal seams to make a long strip; press seams to one side. Press the strip in half, wrong sides together.

Step 4. Stitch the binding to the quilt top with raw edges aligned, overlapping the beginning and end and mitering corners.

Step 5. Turn the binding to the back side and hand-stitch in place.

ADDING THE TOYS

Step 1. Place two lily pad shapes right sides together; stitch all around. Cut a slit in one side; turn right side out through slit to complete one lily pad. Repeat to make four lily pads.

Step 2. Place two bud shapes right sides together; stitch around three sides, leaving the long straight end open. Turn right side out. Repeat to make four buds.

Step 3. Place a bit of fiberfill in the tip of the lily buds. Wrap the toy squeakers in batting from the 10" x 20" batting piece. Insert a squeaker into each bud. Stuff with fiberfill, leaving bottom straight section empty.

Step 4. Cut a slit in the flower shapes as marked on the pattern. Insert the empty end of a bud into the slit in each flower as shown in Figure 5. Flatten the bud end on the back side of the flower, again referring to Figure 5. Pin in place from top of flower.

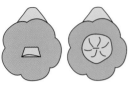

Figure 5   **Figure 6**

Step 5. Stitch around the base of each bud as shown in Figure 6.

Step 6. Place the lily pads in the corners of the G strips with slit side down referring to the Placement Diagram for positioning; pin to hold.

Step 7. Place a flower/bud unit in the center of each lily pad; pin through all layers.

Step 8. Stitch a line along the center of each flower petal through all layers to attach the lily pad/flowers in place as shown in Figure 7.

Figure 7

Step 9. Repeat Steps 2 and 3 with the frog head and toy shaker, leaving 1" at open end empty.

Step 10. Cut a slit in the fleece frog body piece as marked on pattern. Sew the frog body pieces all around with right sides together; cut a slit in the stripe side. Turn right side out.

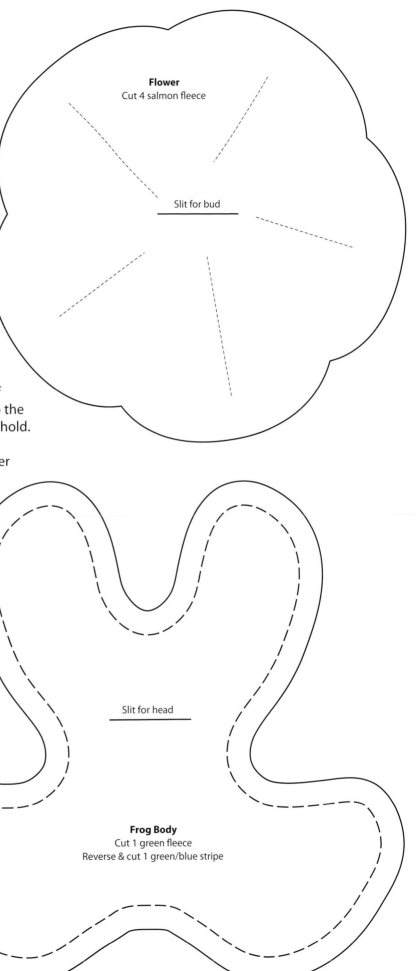

Flower
Cut 4 salmon fleece

Slit for bud

Slit for head

Frog Body
Cut 1 green fleece
Reverse & cut 1 green/blue stripe

Step 11. Insert the empty end of the head piece into the slit in the fleece body side. Stitch around the base of the head piece to hold in place as shown in Figure 8, being careful not to catch the stripe fabric in the stitching.

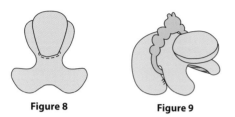

Figure 8   **Figure 9**

Step 12. Firmly stuff the leg sections of the frog body; lightly stuff the body section. Slipstitch the opening in the stripe side closed.

Step 13. Push the back legs through the toy ring, if desired.

Step 14. Hand-stitch the front legs to the back legs to make the crouching frog shape as shown in Figure 9.

Step 15. Glue the black pupil shapes to the white eye shapes. Glue the eyes in place on the frog head. Firmly hand-stitch in place to finish. ●

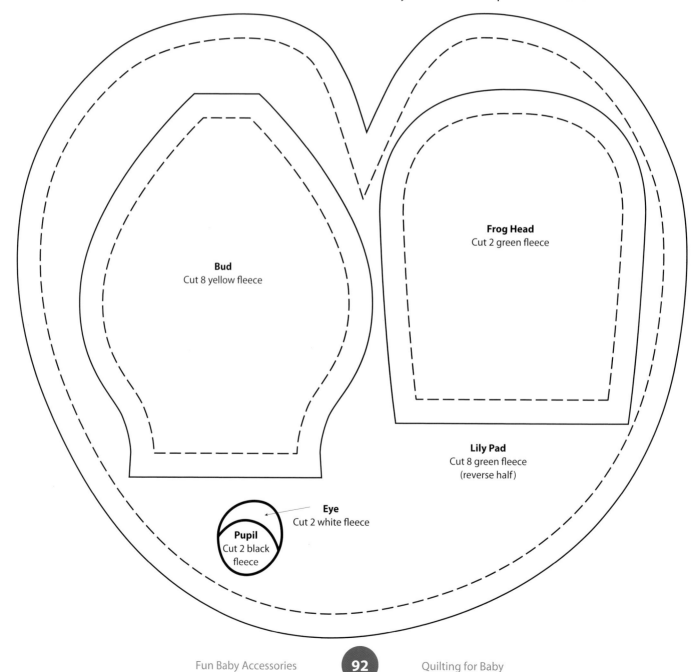

Bud
Cut 8 yellow fleece

Frog Head
Cut 2 green fleece

Lily Pad
Cut 8 green fleece
(reverse half)

Eye
Cut 2 white fleece

Pupil
Cut 2 black fleece

Mom's Forever Tote & Pouch

Designs by Sue Harvey & Sandy Boobar

These versatile bags will take Mom from diapers through sporting events.

PROJECT SPECIFICATIONS
Skill Level: Intermediate/Advanced
Tote Size: 14½" x 11½" x 5½"
Pouch Size: 5½" x 9" x 2½"

QUILTING THE PIECES

Step 1. Apply the fusible fleece pieces to the wrong side of the correspondingly lettered large and small floral, and stripe pieces. For example: fuse Af to A, Bf to B, etc. After fusing, set aside the H piece for tote finishing.

Step 2. Apply the remaining Af fusible fleece pieces to the wrong side of the AA lining pieces; repeat with the remaining Df pieces to the DD pieces, and the remaining Gf piece to the GG piece.

Step 3. Layer the correspondingly lettered lining pieces, fleece sides together with the large and small floral, and stripe pieces. For example: layer AA with A, BB with B, etc. Pin or spray-baste layers to hold.

Step 4. Layer the J and JJ pieces with the 6½" x 27" insulated batting piece; pin or spray-baste layers to hold. Repeat with the K and KK pieces and the 3½" x 10" insulated batting pieces.

Step 5. Using brown all-purpose thread, machine-quilt 1¼" channels along the length of all units as shown in Figure 1; remove pins. ***Note:*** *For A units, 12½" is the length; for B and C units, 10½" is the length.*

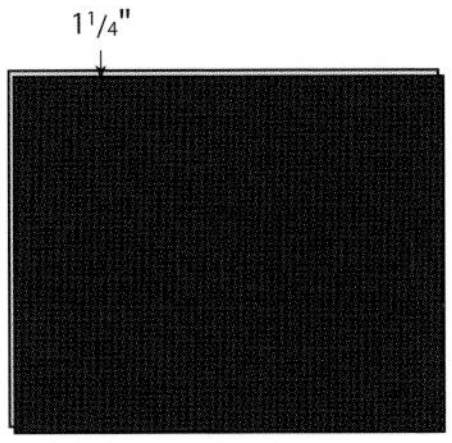

Figure 1

FABRIC Measurements based on 42" usable fabric width except as noted.	#STRIPS & PIECES	CUT	#PIECES	SUBCUT
½ yard aqua/chocolate stripe	1	10½" x 42"	2	15½" B pieces
¾ yard large teal/chocolate floral	1	6½" x 42"	4	7½" E pieces
	1	15½" x 42"	2	10½" C pieces
			1	6½" G piece
⅞ yard teal print	6	3¾" x 42" binding		
	3	1⅜" x 42" L		
1¼ yards small teal/chocolate floral	1	15½" x 42"	2	12½" A pieces
			2	8½" I pieces
	2	6½" x 42"	1	27" J piece
			2	12½" D pieces
			2	4" x 15½" F pieces
	1	6½" x 42" H		
	1	3½" x 42"	2	10" K pieces
1⅝ yard aqua print (lining)	3	6½" x 42"	1	27" JJ piece
			2	12½" DD pieces
			1	15½" GG piece
			4	7½" EE pieces
			2	3½" x 10" KK pieces
	2	15½" x 42"	2	10½" BB pieces
			2	10½" CC pieces
			2	12½" AA pieces
			2	4" FF pieces
1¾ yard 45"-wide fusible fleece	1	15½" x 45"	2	10½" Bf pieces
			2	10½" Cf pieces
	2	12½" x 45"	4	15½" Af pieces
			4	6½" Df pieces
	1	6½" x 45"	2	15½" Gf pieces
	1	6½" x 42" Hf		
	1	4" x 45"	2	15½" Ff pieces

SUPPLIES

- Thin batting 2—2½" x 22"
- Hot/cold insulated batting 1—6½" x 27" and 2—3½" x 10"
- All-purpose thread to match fabrics
- ¼ yard 60"-wide clear vinyl
- Tape
- 3" (¾"-wide) black hook-and-loop tape
- 16"-long black sports zipper
- Basting spray
- Basic sewing tools and supplies

COMPLETING THE POCKETS

Step 1. Press under ¼" on one 15½" edge of each I piece; press under ¼" again. Topstitch to hem.

Step 2. Mark a line across the 15½" width of each A unit 2" from the bottom edge on the lining side as shown in Figure 2.

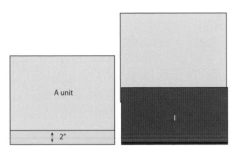

Figure 2

Step 3. Align the unhemmed edge of each I piece with the marked line, placing the I pieces right sides together with the lining, again referring to Figure 2. Stitch in place using a ¼" seam allowance.

Step 4. Press the I pieces up; pin in place. Machine-baste along the outer edges.

Step 5. Prepare template for the B/C Curve. Layer the C units right sides up; trim the upper left corners as shown in Figure 3.

Figure 3

Step 6. Layer the B units right sides up; flip the template and trim the upper right corners, again referring to Figure 3.

Step 7. Press ¼" under on one long edge of each L strip.

Step 8. Align the unpressed edge of a strip with the curved raw edge of a B unit; stitch the L strip in place. Trim even with the B unit. Fold the strip to the lining side of B; pin to hold. Hand-stitch in place to bind edge.

Step 9. Repeat Step 8 with the remaining B unit and both C units.

Step 10. Layer the E and EE pieces with wrong sides together; pin to hold. Repeat Step 8 on one 7½" edge of each E unit.

Step 11. Gather the bottom 7½" edge of each E unit to measure 6½"; stay-stitch to hold.

Step 12. Measure 6¾" down from the top edge of each D unit and mark a line across the 6½" width as shown in Figure 4. Align the gathered edge of an E unit with the marked line, again referring to Figure 4. Stitch in place. Press up and pin to hold.

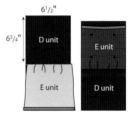

Figure 4   **Figure 5**

Step 13. Align the remaining E units at the bottom edges of the D units; pin in place.

Step 14. Machine-baste pockets in place on D along the outer edges.

Step 15. Layer a B and C unit on each A unit as shown in Figure 5; pin to hold. Mark a line down the center of the layered units, again referring to Figure 5.

Step 16. Stitch on the marked lines to separate the B and C units into pockets and the I pieces on the lining side of A into two pockets as shown in Figure 6.

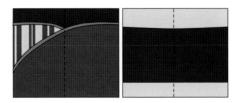

Figure 6

Step 17. Machine-baste along outer edges to hold in place.

COMPLETING THE TOTE
Step 1. Separate the zipper halves.

Step 2. Place the opening edge of one zipper half right sides together with one F unit with the first zipper tooth ¾" from the end as shown in Figure 7; stitch ¼" from the zipper teeth. Repeat with the second F unit and zipper half. *Note: The other end of the zipper will extend off the F unit.*

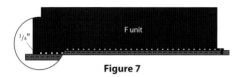

Figure 7

Step 3. Fold the F units down, aligning the folded edge along the edge of the zipper teeth as shown in Figure 8; pin in place. Topstitch ⅛" from folded edge and then ¼" from the stitched line, again referring to Figure 8.

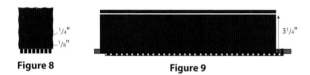

Figure 8   **Figure 9**

Step 4. Trim each unit to 3¼" wide as shown in Figure 9; zip the halves together to complete the F/zipper unit.

Step 5. Fold one long edge of the H piece 1½" to the fleece side and press as shown in Figure 10; fold the remaining long edge ½" to the fleece side and press, again referring to Figure 10.

Figure 10   **Figure 11**

Step 6. Measure 21" along length of the H strip to find the center and mark. Center the two 2½" x 22" batting pieces in the marked center of the H strip, inserting the edge under the 1½" folded edge as shown in Figure 11. *Note: This adds extra padding in the shoulder area of the strap.*

Step 7. Bring the folded long edge over the batting to cover the raw edge of the opposite long edge as shown in Figure 12; press. Pin to hold.

Figure 12   **Figure 13**

Step 8. Topstitch along the center folded edge as shown in Figure 13; stitch 1" on each side of the center stitching to complete the strap.

Step 9. Join the binding strips on short ends with a diagonal seam to make a long strip; press seams open. Press the strip in half with wrong sides together to complete the binding.

Step 10. Place a D-E unit lining sides together with one end of the G unit as shown in Figure 14; stitch using a ½" seam allowance. *Note: Use a ½" seam allowance for all remaining steps for the tote.*

Figure 14

Step 11. Repeat with the second D-E unit on the remaining end of the G unit.

Step 12. Bind the seam allowance edges of the D-E-G unit as for the edges of the B and C units in Step 8 of Completing the Pockets.

Step 13. Sew an A-B-C unit lining sides together with one edge of the D-E-G unit; repeat with the second A-B-C unit on the opposite edge of the D-E-G unit.

Step 14. Bind the edges of the pieced unit, enclosing previous binding ends.

Step 15. Set the F/zipper unit into the top of the pieced unit.

Step 16. Center the H strap right sides together on each D-E end of the pieced unit as shown in Figure 15; pin in place.

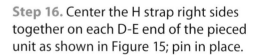

Figure 15

Step 17. Bind the top edge to complete the tote.

COMPLETING THE INSULATED POUCH
Note: Use a ½" seam allowance for all steps for the pouch.

Step 1. Cut one 6½" x 27" and two 3½" x 10" pieces clear vinyl.

Step 2. Place the longer piece on the lining side of the J unit and the shorter pieces on the lining side of each K unit. Tape in place to hold, if necessary.

Step 3. Place a K unit lining sides together at one end of the J unit as shown in Figure 16.

Figure 16

Step 4. Stitch along three edges of the K unit as shown in Figure 17.

Figure 17

Step 5. Repeat Steps 3 and 4 with the second K unit.

Step 6. Cut two 32"-long binding pieces.

Step 7. Bind edges along 6" of the front J-K seams, using separate binding pieces as shown in Figure 18.

Figure 18

Figure 19

Step 8. Bind around top of J-K opening.

Step 9. Bind the remaining edges of the pouch.

Step 10. Sew the hook piece of the hook-and-loop tape 1¾" from the opening edge of the pouch as shown in Figure 19. Sew the loop piece along the binding edge on the inside of the pouch flap piece, again referring to Figure 19, to complete the pouch. ●

Insulated Pouch
Placement Diagram 5½" x 9" x 2½"

B/C Curve
Trim C units
Reverse & trim B units

Mom's Forever Tote
Placement Diagram 14½" x 11½" x 5½"

Little Lamb Baby Quilt

Design by Chris Malone

Appliquéd lambs and flowers in pink stand out on the white background of this cute little baby quilt.

PROJECT SPECIFICATIONS

Skill Level: Beginner
Quilt Size: 20" x 20"
Block Size: 6¾" x 6¾"
Number of Blocks: 4

Little Lamb
6¾" x 6¾" Block
Make 1 & 1 reversed

Flower
6¾" x 6¾" Block
Make 1 & 1 reversed

FABRIC Measurements based on 42" usable fabric width.	#STRIPS & PIECES	CUT	#PIECES	SUBCUT
Scraps pink/white check, pink check and green tonal		Appliqué pieces as per patterns		
⅓ yard green/pink floral	2	3⅜" x 42"	14	3⅜" E squares
⅜ yard green mini dot	3	1" x 42"	6	7¼" B strips
			3	15½" C strips
	3	2¼" x 42" binding		
½ yard white tonal	1	7¼" x 42"	4	7¼" A squares
	2	3⅜" x 42"	14	3⅜" D squares
Backing		26" x 26"		

SUPPLIES

- Batting 26" x 26"
- All-purpose thread to match fabrics
- Quilting thread
- Green embroidery floss
- ½ yard 12"-wide fusible web
- ½ yard fabric stabilizer
- 12 (¼") dark pink buttons
- 2 (¾"–1") white plastic rings
- Basic sewing tools and supplies and air-soluble pen

COMPLETING THE BLOCKS

Step 1. Trace the lamb and flower pieces onto the paper side of the fusible web referring to patterns; cut out shapes, leaving a margin around each one.

Step 2. Fuse shapes to the wrong side of fabrics as directed on patterns; cut out shapes on traced lines. Remove paper backing.

Step 3. Arrange lamb and flower motifs on A squares in numerical order referring to pattern motifs for positioning; fuse shapes in place.

Step 4. Cut four 7" x 7" squares fabric stabilizer; pin a square to the wrong side of each fused block.

Step 5. Stitch around each fused shape using thread to match fabrics and a machine blanket stitch. When stitching is complete, remove fabric stabilizer.

Step 6. Transfer the ground line under each lamb with the air-soluble pen; outline-stitch on the marked line using 2 strands green embroidery floss to complete the blocks.

COMPLETING THE QUILT

Step 1. Join one Little Lamb and one Flower block with three B strips to make a row; press seams toward B strips. Repeat to make two rows, referring to the Placement Diagram for positioning of blocks.

Step 2. Join the rows with three C strips; press seams toward C strips.

Step 3. Draw a diagonal line from corner to corner on the wrong side of each D square.

Step 4. Place a D square right sides together with an E square, and referring to Figure 1, sew ¼" on each side of the marked line. Cut apart on the marked line and press open with seam toward E to complete two D-E units. Repeat with all D and E squares to complete 28 total D-E units.

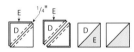

Figure 1

Step 5. Join six D-E units as shown in Figure 2 to make a side row; press seams in one direction. Repeat to make two side rows.

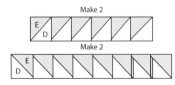

Figure 2

Step 6. Sew the side rows to opposite sides of the pieced center referring to the Placement Diagram for positioning; press seams toward B strips.

Step 7. Join eight D-E units to make the top row, again referring to Figure 2; repeat to make the bottom row. Press seams in one direction. Sew these rows to the top and bottom of the pieced center to complete the pieced top. Press seams toward C strips.

Step 8. Finish the quilt referring to the Finishing Instructions on page 173.

Step 9. Sew two buttons to lamb faces for eyes and four buttons on each flower center. Sew a white plastic ring to each top back side corner for hanging to complete the quilt. ●

Little Lamb Baby Quilt
Placement Diagram 20" x 20"

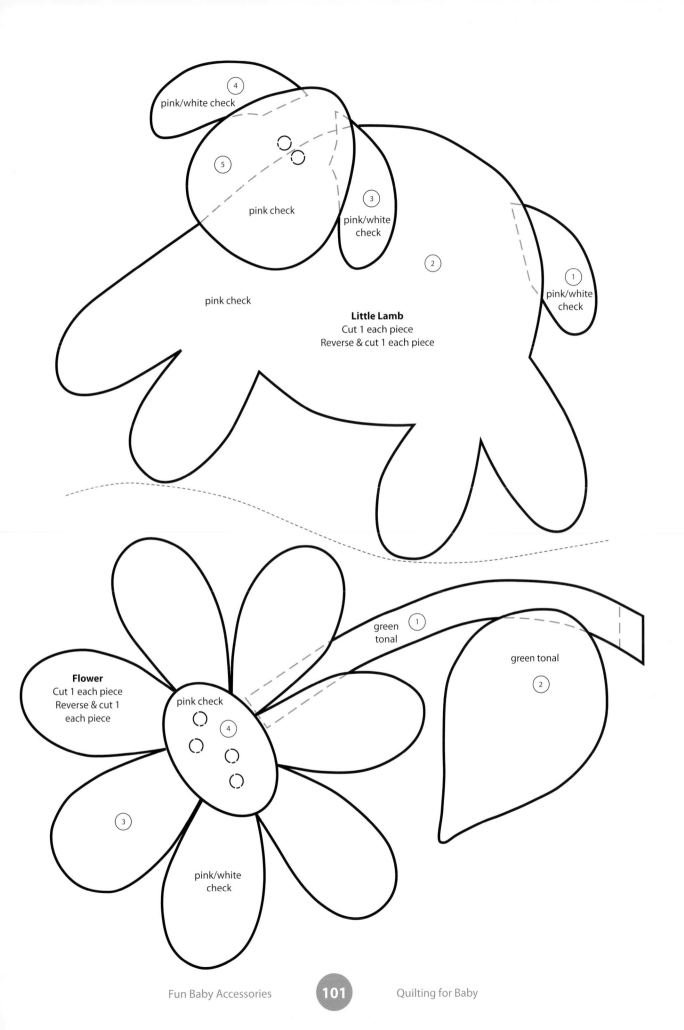

Little Lamb
Cut 1 each piece
Reverse & cut 1 each piece

pink/white check

4

5

pink check

3

pink/white
check

2

1

pink/white
check

pink check

pink check

Flower
Cut 1 each piece
Reverse & cut 1
each piece

pink check

4

3

pink/white
check

green
tonal

1

green tonal

2

Hugs & Kisses Play Quilt

Design by Jenny Foltz

Bright primary colors attract the attention of Baby during playtime.

PROJECT SPECIFICATIONS
Skill Level: Intermediate
Quilt Size: 40" x 40"
Block Size: 8" x 8"
Number of Blocks: 9

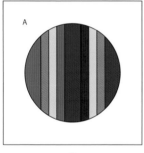

O
8" x 8" Block
Make 5

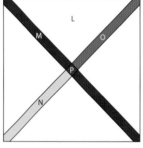

X
8" x 8" Block
Make 4

COMPLETING THE STRIP SETS & UNITS

Step 1. Join one each C, D, E, F, G, H and I strips with right sides together along length referring to Figure 1 for order of piecing; press seams in one direction.

Figure 1

Figure 2

Step 2. Cut two 5½" W1 circles, two 4½" Q squares and two 4½" diagonal R squares (aligning seams with the 45-degree-angle line on your rotary ruler) from the strip set referring to Figure 2.

FABRIC Measurements based on 42" usable fabric width.	#STRIPS & PIECES	CUT	#PIECES	SUBCUT
⅛ yard orange tonal	1	1½" x 42" G		
	2	1" x 42" J		
½ yard red tonal	2	1" x 42"	8	7" M strips
	1	4½" x 42"	2	8½" B4 strips
	2	1" x 32½" S		
	1	2" x 42" E		
	1	1" x 42" K		
⅝ yard green tonal	1	4½" x 42"	3	8½" B2 strips
	1	7" x 42"	1	6½" O strip
	1	2" x 42" I		
	3	1" x 42" C		
⅝ yard yellow tonal	1	4½" x 42"	4	8½" B3 strips
	2	1" x 32½" T		
	1	7" x 42"	1	6½" N strip
	3	1" x 42" F		
⅞ yard white tonal	1	7⅞" x 42"	4	7⅞" squares; cut on both diagonals to make 16 L triangles
	2	8½" x 42"	5	8½" A squares
1¼ yards blue tonal	1	4½" x 42"	3	8½" B1 strips
	4	4" x 32½" U		
	5	2¼" x 42" binding		
	1	1½" x 42"	1	6½" P strip
	1	1" x 42" D		
	3	1½" x 42" H		
Backing		46" x 46"		

SUPPLIES

- Batting 46" x 46"
- Neutral color and multicolored all-purpose thread
- Quilting thread
- ½ yard 18"-wide fusible web
- ⅝ yard fabric stabilizer
- 5½"-diameter plate or circle template
- Basic sewing tools and supplies

Step 4. Using multicolored thread and a zigzag stitch, stitch around each circle to hold in place and complete the O blocks; remove fabric stabilizer.

COMPLETING THE X BLOCKS

Step 1. Join two L triangles with one M strip matching at straight ends as shown in Figure 5; press seams toward M. Repeat to make eight L-M units.

Figure 5

Step 2. Sew the P strip between the N and O strips with right sides together along length to make an N-O-P strip set; press seams toward N and O strips.

Step 3. Subcut the N-O-P strip set into four 1" N-O-P units as shown in Figure 6.

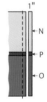

Figure 6

Step 3. Join two each C, F, H and J strips and one K strip with right sides together along length to make a strip set referring to Figure 3 for order of piecing; press seams in one direction.

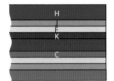

Figure 3

Step 4. Cut three 5½" W2 circles and four 4½" V squares from the strip set referring to Figure 4.

Figure 4

COMPLETING THE O BLOCKS

Step 1. Cut five 5½" circles from the fusible web; fuse a circle to the wrong side of each W1 and W2 circle; remove paper backing.

Step 2. Center a circle on each A square and fuse in place. *Note: Place one W2 circle diagonally on the A square referring to the center block in the Placement Diagram.*

Step 3. Cut five 8" squares fabric stabilizer; pin a square to the wrong side of each fused A square.

Step 4. To complete one X block, join two L-M units with an N-O-P unit as shown in Figure 7; press seams in one direction.

Figure 7

Step 5. Trim excess at corners using a straightedge as shown in Figure 8 to complete one X block.

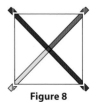

Figure 8

Step 6. Repeat Steps 4 and 5 to complete four X blocks.

COMPLETING THE QUILT

Step 1. Join two O blocks with one X block, and one each B1 and B2 strip to make Row 1 as shown in Figure 9; press seams away from blocks. Repeat to make Row 3, alternating placement of the W1 and W2 circles.

Step 2. Join two X blocks with one O block, and one each B1 and B2 strip to make Row 2, again referring to Figure 9; press seams away from blocks.

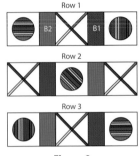

Figure 9

Step 3. Join Q and R squares with one B4 and two B3 strips to make a sashing row as shown in Figure 10; press seams toward B3 and B4 strips. Repeat to make two sashing rows.

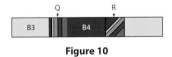

Figure 10

Step 4. Join the block rows with the sashing rows referring to the Placement Diagram to complete the pieced center; press seams toward the sashing rows.

Step 5. Sew an S strip to a U strip; press seams toward U. Repeat to make two S-U strips.

Step 6. Sew an S-U strip to opposite sides of the pieced center referring to the Placement Diagram for positioning; press seams toward the S-U strips.

Step 7. Sew a T strip to a U strip; press seams toward U. Repeat to make two T-U strips.

Step 8. Sew a pieced V square to each end of each T-U strip; press seams away from V.

Step 9. Sew a T-U-V strip to the top and bottom of the pieced center to complete the top; press seams toward the T-U-V strips.

Step 10. Finish the quilt referring to the Finishing Instructions on page 173. ●

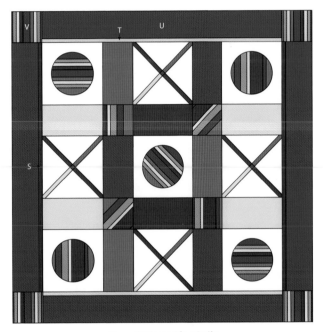

Hugs & Kisses Play Quilt
Placement Diagram 40" x 40"

Baby Welcome Wall Quilt

Design by Christine Schultz

Paper-pieced blocks combine with a welcome banner to make a fabric birth announcement.

PROJECT SPECIFICATIONS
Skill Level: Intermediate
Quilt Size: 23" x 15¼"
Block Sizes: 5½" x 4⅜", 4" x 4, 3½" x 5⅝" and 3½" x 6¾"
Number of Blocks: 1, 1, 1 and 2

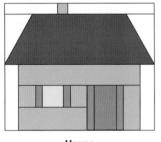

House
5½" x 4⅜" Block
Make 1

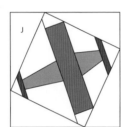

Airplane
4" x 4" Block
Make 1

Tree 1
3½" x 5⅝" Block
Make 1

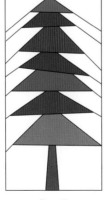

Tree 2
3½" x 6¾" Block
Make 2

FABRIC Measurements based on 42" usable fabric width.	#STRIPS & PIECES	CUT	#PIECES	SUBCUT
Scraps brown, blue, rust, gold, tan, greens, light and dark gray, black and beige		Paper-piecing as directed on patterns		
3" x 13¼" K strip white solid				
½ yard dark blue print	2	2½" x 42"	2	2½" x 11¾" H
	3	2¼" x 42" binding	2	2½" x 23½" I
⅝ yard cream print	1	6" x 2⅞" A		
	1	4" x 1⅝" B		
	2	1½" x 7¼" C		
	1	4" x 4½" D		
	1	4½" x 11" E		
		Paper-piecing as directed on patterns		
		J pieces as per template		
⅔ yard border stripe	2	1" x 12" F along length		
	2	1" x 20" G along length		
Backing		29" x 22"		

SUPPLIES
- Batting 29" x 22"
- Neutral color all-purpose thread
- Quilting thread
- Black, tan, dark gold, red, green and orange embroidery floss
- Water-erasable marker or pencil
- Basic sewing tools and supplies

COMPLETING THE BLOCKS
Step 1. Set machine to a short stitch length to make removal of paper easier.

Step 2. Prepare copies of full-size paper-piecing patterns. Cut fabric pieces to fit sections of patterns referring to patterns for fabric colors.

Step 3. To begin House block, place piece 1 right side up on the unmarked side of the house paper-piecing pattern, covering the piece 1 section and extending ¼" into all surrounding sections. Place piece 2 right sides together with piece 1 on the 1-2 seam side as shown in Figure 1; turn paper over and stitch on the marked 1-2 line, again referring to Figure 1.

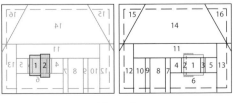

Figure 1

Step 4. Press piece 2 to the right side as shown in Figure 2.

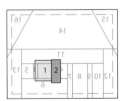

Figure 2

Step 5. Repeat Steps 3 and 4 with remaining pieces in numerical order.

Step 6. Trim finished foundation along outside-edge line to complete the unit.

Step 7. Repeat Steps 3–6 with the chimney section paper-piecing pattern.

Step 8. Sew the chimney section to the house section to complete the House block.

Step 9. Repeat Steps 3–6 to complete one Tree 1 block and two Tree 2 blocks.

Step 10. Repeat Steps 3–6 to complete one Airplane unit. Sew a J triangle to each side to complete the Airplane block.

COMPLETING THE QUILT

Step 1. Sew A to the top of the House block and B to the top of the Tree 1 block; press seams toward A and B.

Step 2. Join one each House and Tree 1 and two Tree 2 blocks with two C strips to make a row as shown in Figure 3; press seams toward Tree 1 and C.

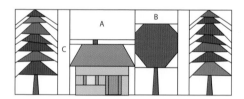

Figure 3

Step 3. Join the Airplane block with D and E pieces to make a row as shown in Figure 4; press seams toward D and E.

Figure 4

Step 4. Join the two rows to complete the pieced center; press seam toward the E-D-Airplane row.

Step 5. Center and sew F strips to opposite sides and G strips to the top and bottom of the pieced center, stopping stitching ¼" from the end of each seam; press seams toward F and G.

Step 6. Miter corners referring to Figure 5; press miter seam open.

Figure 5

Step 7. Sew H strips to opposite ends and I strips to the top and bottom of the pieced center; press seams toward H and I strips.

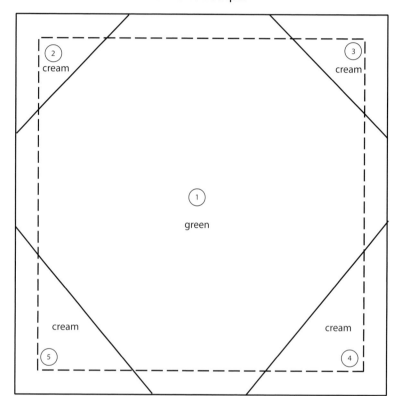

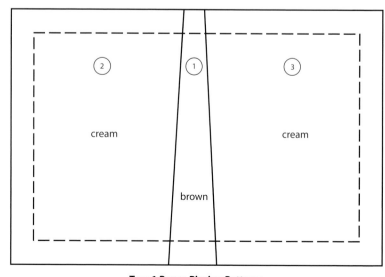

Tree 1 Paper-Piecing Patterns
Make 1 copy of each

Step 8. Using 2 strands black embroidery floss, straight-stitch two straight lines from the tail of the Airplane about 1" long and 1⅛" apart at the ends.

Step 9. Mark swing pattern below Tree 1 using a water-erasable marker or pencil and referring to the Placement Diagram for positioning. Straight-stitch the ropes using 2 strands tan embroidery floss and the seat using 4 strands dark gold embroidery floss.

Step 10. Finish the quilt referring to the Finishing Instructions on page 173.

Step 11. Fold and crease the K strip along the length to mark the center.

Step 12. Using a water-erasable marker or pencil, draw a straight line ½" from the creased long edge as shown in Figure 6; hand-print the word Welcome, the baby's name and date of birth along the line. Transfer the star shapes given on page 111 randomly on the strip.

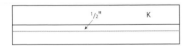

Figure 6

Step 13. Straight-stitch the marked word lines using 2 strands black embroidery floss.

Step 14. Using 2 strands red, green or orange embroidery floss, straight-stitch star designs.

Step 15. Fold the stitched strip along length with right sides together; stitch across the right end and along the long edge to make a tube. Turn right side out; press.

Step 16. Pull threads on the left end to make a short fringe.

Step 17. Hand-tack the banner at the ends of the embroidered lines at the tail of the airplane and toward the left edge of the quilt, tacking in several spots along the way to finish. ●

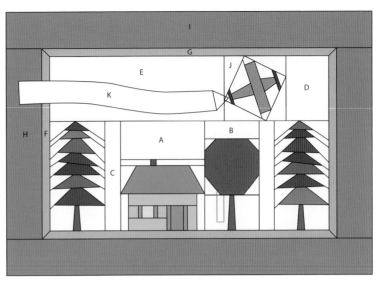

Baby Welcome Wall Quilt
Placement Diagram 23" x 15¼"

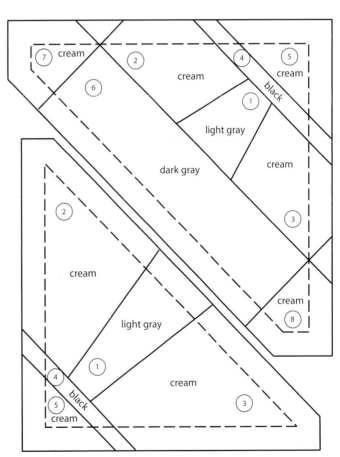

Airplane Paper-Piecing Patterns
Make 1 copy of each

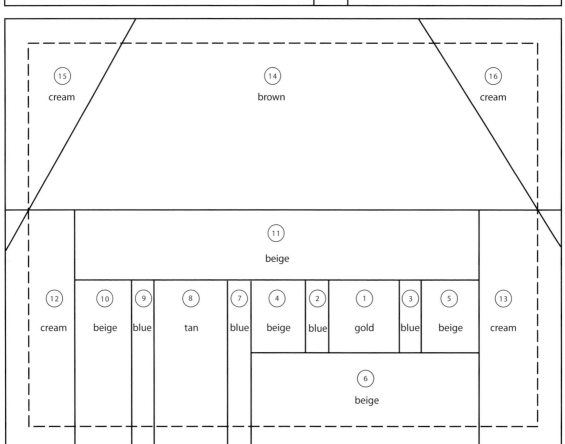

| 2 cream | 1 rust | 3 cream |

| 15 cream | 14 brown | 16 cream |

11
beige

| 12 cream | 10 beige | 9 blue | 8 tan | 7 blue | 4 beige | 2 blue | 1 gold | 3 blue | 5 beige | 13 cream |

6
beige

House Paper-Piecing Patterns
Make 1 copy of each

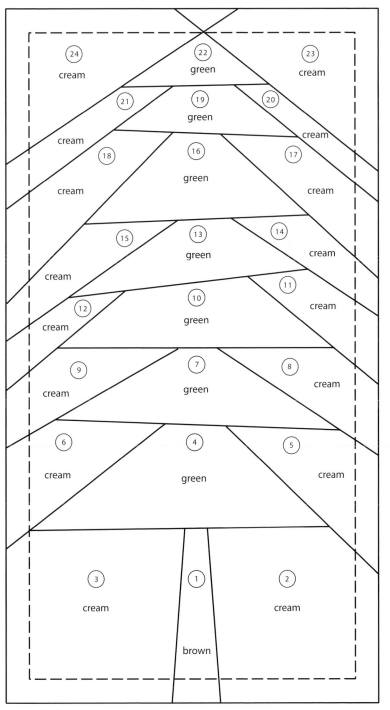

Tree 2 Paper-Piecing Pattern
Make 2 copies

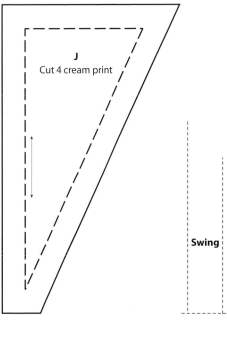

J
Cut 4 cream print

Swing

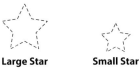

Large Star   **Small Star**

Stroller Buddy Pack

Design by Jodi G. Warner

Make a classy bag to attach to the back of a stroller to hold baby bottles, water bottles, keys and lots of other essentials.

PROJECT SPECIFICATIONS
Skill Level: Advanced
Bag Size: 13½" x 5¾" x 4"

COMPLETING THE UNITS
Note: *Use a ¼" seam allowance throughout this section.*

Step 1. Mark a diagonal line from corner to corner on the wrong side of each B square.

Step 2. Place a B square right sides together on one corner of A and stitch on the marked line as shown in Figure 1; trim seam to ¼" and press seam toward B as shown in Figure 2.

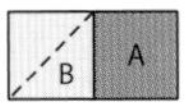

Figure 1   **Figure 2**

Step 3. Repeat Step 2 on the remaining end of A as shown in Figure 3 to complete one A-B unit; repeat to complete 14 A-B units.

  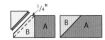

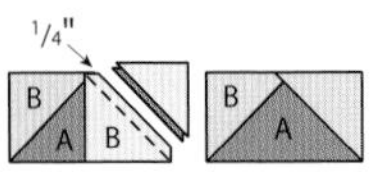

Figure 3 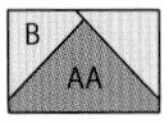   **Figure 4** 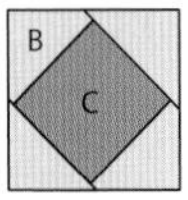   **Figure 5**

Step 4. Repeat Steps 2 and 3 with AA and B to complete two AA-B units as shown in Figure 4.

Step 5. Sew B to each corner of C as in Step 2 to complete one B-C unit as shown in Figure 5.

FABRIC Measurements based on 42" usable fabric width.	#STRIPS & PIECES	CUT	#PIECES	SUBCUT
⅛ yard cream solid	2	1¼" x 42"	36	1¼" B squares
⅛ yard dark rose solid	1	2" x 42"	2	1½" AA rectangles
			14	1¼" A rectangles
			1	2" C square
⅛ yard dark green solid	1	1¼" x 42"	2	14½" D strips
½ yard green/rose/beige stripe (60"-wide upholstery fabric used in sample)	1	6¾" x 42"	1	14½" E rectangle
			1	14½" F rectangle
			2	5" I rectangles
	1	6½" x 42"	1	14½" G rectangle
			1	5" x 14½" H rectangle
1 yard beige solid to coordinate with stripe for lining and inside pouches	1	6¾" x 42"	1	14½" E lining
			1	14½" F lining
			2	5" I lining
	1	10½" x 42"	2	17" J rectangles
			2	3" x 8⅝" K rectangles
	1	5" x 42"	1	14½" H lining
			1	16¼" M rectangle
		L pieces as per template		

SUPPLIES
- All-purpose thread to match fabrics
- 1¼ yards ⅜"-wide dark green grosgrain ribbon
- 4 yards 1"-wide golden tan woven strapping
- 1 (9") beige zipper
- ½ yard heavy stiffener (Timtex brand)
- 10" golden tan ⅝"-wide hook-and-loop tape
- 4 strap adjusters for 1" strapping
- 2 cord stops
- Basic sewing tools and supplies

COMPLETING THE PIECED STRIP

Note: Use a ¼" seam allowance throughout this section.

Step 1. Join seven A-B units as shown in Figure 6 to make an A-B strip; press seams in one direction. Repeat to make two strips.

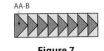

Figure 6   **Figure 7**

Step 2. Add an AA-B unit to one end of each A-B strip as shown in Figure 7; press seams in same direction.

Step 3. Join the A-B strips with the B-C unit to make the A-B-C strip as shown in Figure 8; press seams toward the B-C unit.

Figure 8

Step 4. Sew D strips to opposite long edges of the A-B-C strip as shown in Figure 9; press seams toward D strips.

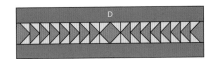

Figure 9

Step 5. Fold and press the long raw edge of each D strip ½" to the wrong side to make D finish at ½".

COMPLETING THE POCKET PANEL

Note: Use a ½" seam allowance throughout this section.

Step 1. Fold the G pocket panel in half along the length with wrong sides together; mark pocket stitching lines on the folded piece as shown in Figure 10. Reinforce stitching.

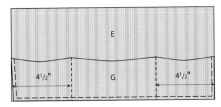

Figure 10

Step 2. Place the folded G piece on the right side of E with side and bottom raw edges aligned, again referring to Figure 10; baste edges. Stitch from the lower raw edge to the folded edge on pocket stitching lines, again referring to Figure 10.

Step 3. Position and pin the A-B-C-D strip ¼" above pocket and ¾" from top edge of E as shown in Figure 11; baste across panel ends.

Step 4. Topstitch along outer edges of D with matching thread to finish pocket panel.

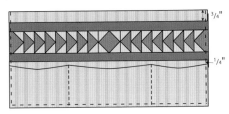

Figure 11

COMPLETING THE BOX BODY

Note: Use a ½" seam allowance throughout this section.

Step 1. Mark a dot at the ½" seam allowance intersections at the lower corners of F and I outer and lining pieces, the pocket panel and the E lining piece; and at all corners of the H outer and lining pieces.

Step 2. For better lining fit, taper-trim side edges of linings E, F and I so they remain at the original cut size at the top edge and ⅛" smaller at the lower edge as shown in Figure 12. Taper-trim ⅛" from all four edges at corners of lining piece H.

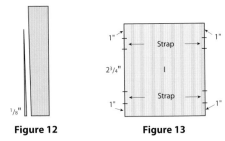

Figure 12   **Figure 13**

Step 3. Mark strap openings on the 6¾" edges of the I pieces as shown in Figure 13. *Note: Side straps will support the main box by passing through openings at side edges of front and back box panels, and between main fabric and lining. Strapping is stitched in place through box layers.*

Step 4. With right sides together, join the outer F and I pieces with the pocket panel at side edges to make the box frame as shown in Figure 14, stopping and locking stitches at each side of the marked strap openings, and at lower-edge dots. Join E, F and I lining pieces in a similar manner to make box frame lining except do not leave strap openings; press seams open.

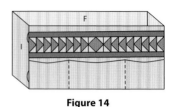

Figure 14

Step 5. Inset H at lower edges of box frame, stopping and locking stitching at corners; repeat process for H lining inside lining box frame. Press seams open as far as possible to create box shaping. Press upper opening edges to the wrong side ½" on outer shell and lining. Turn outer shell right side out.

Step 6. Cut two 32" back straps, two 24" front straps and four 6½" upper straps from strapping. *Note: Straps are sized to be adjustable for most stroller styles. Standard distance between side bars is 17" or 18". Modify strap lengths for specific stroller with which this pack will be used.*

Step 7. Sew 5" lengths of loop fastener strips to two of the upper strap pieces and 1½" lengths of hook fastener strips to the remaining upper strap pieces as shown in Figure 15. Stitch a double ¼" hem at end of all four strips. Layer each loop strip with a hook strip and baste unhemmed ends as shown in Figure 16.

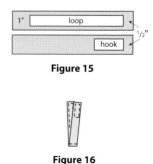

Figure 15

Figure 16

Step 8. Insert front and back straps in appropriate positions through side seam openings of outer shell as shown in Figure 17; center and baste in place. Double-stitch seams at strap openings to hold straps in place and close openings.

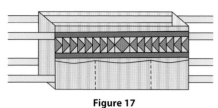

Figure 17

Step 9. Cut stiffener panels: two front/back 5½ x 13¼", two side 3¾" x 5½" and one bottom 3¾" x 13¼". Insert into appropriate positions inside outer shell between shell and straps; insert lining.

Step 10. Align upper folded edges of lining and shell, matching side seams. Position joined ends of hook-and-loop strap sets between the shell and lining backs, approximately 2⅜" in from side seams as shown in Figure 18; stitch close to edge all around top, catching straps in stitching. Reinforce stitching across straps.

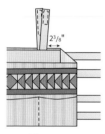

Figure 18

Step 11. Align main and lining side seams, then connect side layers by stitching from back straps to front straps as shown in Figure 19. Connect front layers by stitching in the ditch of seams of the A-B-C pieced strip.

Figure 19

Step 12. Follow strap-adjuster package directions to attach adjusters to front straps. Stitch double ¼" hems on back strap ends.

COMPLETING THE DRAWSTRING POUCHES

Note: Use a ½" seam allowance throughout this section.

Step 1. To complete one pouch, press vertical creases 2½" and 6½" in from side edges of J as shown in Figure 20.

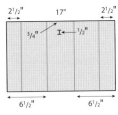

Figure 20

Step 2. Mark a scant ½" buttonhole opening in center of J ¾" from top edge, again referring to Figure 20. Stitch a buttonhole; cut open.

Step 3. Align side edges right sides together and stitch seam; press seam open. Serge or zigzag raw edges.

Step 4. Bring lower edges together, matching center and seam as shown in Figure 21; fold side edges in to meet the center seam, again referring to Figure 21. Stitch across; serge or zigzag-stitch raw edges to finish pouch bottom.

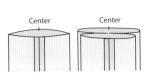

Figure 21　　　　　　**Figure 22**

Step 5. Turn right side out and arrange bottom so that pouch can sit flat; fold along each previously creased line. Edge-stitch along creased lines about 7" down from top edge as shown in Figure 22. Press ¼" under along top edge; press under ½" again and stitch to form cord channel and hem.

Step 6. Cut 20" length of ribbon and insert into casing through the buttonhole. Overlap ends and topstitch together. Trim ends into a point.

Step 7. Follow cord-stop package instructions to insert ribbon ends through opening. Tie ends in a knot.

Step 8. Repeat Steps 1–7 to make the second drawstring pouch.

COMPLETING THE ZIPPER POUCH

Note: Use a ½" seam allowance throughout this section.

Step 1. Serge or zigzag-stitch one long edge of each K strip; fold ½" to the wrong side.

Step 2. Position zipper's metal stop ⅝" from end of folded edge; topstitch folded edges along each side of zipper teeth as shown in Figure 23.

 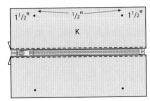

Figure 23　　　　　　**Figure 24**

Step 3. Trim zipper panel to 5" wide with zipper centered. Mark a dot 1½" from each end and ½" from long edge of each K piece to mark corners as shown in Figure 24.

Step 4. Mark corner positions on M at the ½" seam allowance as shown in Figure 25. Stitch ends of M to K as shown in Figure 26; press toward M.

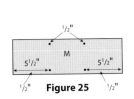

Figure 25　　　　　　**Figure 26**

Step 5. Topstitch next to seam on M, again referring to Figure 26; stay-stitch the long edges of M/K at a scant ½". Clip almost to stitching of K between dots.

Step 6. Transfer corner and M/K seam dots to L, referring to the L template for positioning. Attach L at M/K raw-edge openings, aligning M/K seam dots with M/K seams and matching corresponding corner dots on L and M, and flexing K edge to match L curve. For reinforcement, lock stitching at each corner.

Step 7. Serge or zigzag-stitch raw edges.

Step 8. Turn right side out; work corners out to full size and press seam to shape pouch.

Step 9. Cut a 4" length of ribbon; insert through zipper pull. Overlap ends and topstitch together to make a loop.

POUCH & BOX ASSEMBLY

Step 1. Arrange drawstring and zipper pouches side by side, aligning corners and touching surfaces. Pin, then machine-tack layers together approximately 4" from bottom.

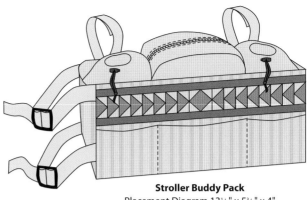

Stroller Buddy Pack
Placement Diagram 13½" x 5¾" x 4"

Step 2. Insert pouch assembly into box, aligning corners and touching surfaces; pin, then machine-tack as for pouches. *Note: Suggested tacking positions: front surface in-the-ditch at lower D strip seamline; back surface at center and under straps approximately 1¼" below upper edge.*

Step 3. Position pack with pieced panel visible from stroller front; lock and secure upper straps around push handle at convenient level.

Step 4. Loop and secure side straps with adjusters snugly around handlebar supports to make ready for storage of needed items. ●

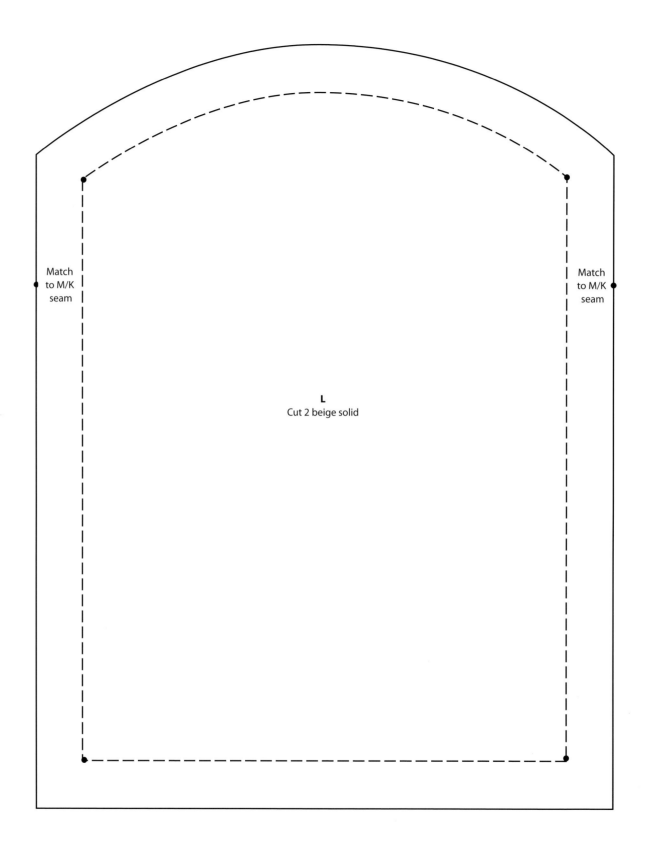

Match to M/K seam

Match to M/K seam

L
Cut 2 beige solid

Teddy Bear Frame

Design by Mary Ayres

Show off your little one in a fabric frame with a 3-D bear.

PROJECT SPECIFICATIONS

Skill Level: Beginner
Frame Size: 8" x 8"

COMPLETING THE FRAME

Step 1. Sew A to B and C to D; press seams open.

Step 2. Join the A-B unit with the C-D unit as shown in Figure 1; press seam open.

Figure 1   **Figure 2**

Step 3. Topstitch ¼" from each seam as shown in Figure 2.

Step 4. Baste interfacing to wrong side of pieced square; pin white muslin square on top of the right side of the pieced fabric square; center and lightly draw a 3½" square on the white muslin with a pencil referring to Figure 3.

Figure 3   **Figure 4**

Step 5. Sew along drawn lines; cut out ¼" from the stitched line on the inside of the stitched square as shown in Figure 4.

FABRIC / SUPPLIES

FABRIC Measurements based on 42" usable fabric width.	#STRIPS & PIECES	CUT
Scrap blue tonal	1	4" A square
Scrap green check	1	5" x 4" B rectangle
Scrap pink print	1	4" x 5" C rectangle
	1	8½" E square
Scrap pink dot	1	5" D square
Scrap white muslin	1	8½" lining square
Scrap white wool felt		Cut as directed on patterns

SUPPLIES

- White all-purpose thread
- 10" (⅜") wooden dowel
- 14" (⅝"-wide) pink dot grosgrain ribbon
- 9" (⅜"-wide) pink check ribbon
- 4½" square clear plastic
- Polyester fiberfill
- Hand drill with ⁷⁄₁₆" bit
- 8½" square firm interfacing
- 1 skein bright blue embroidery floss
- Black No. 12 pearl cotton
- 16" length bright blue baby rickrack
- 2 light blue ⁹⁄₁₆" buttons
- Soft lead pencil
- Basic sewing tools and supplies
- 4½"-square baby photo

Step 6. Clip into corners of the cut area and turn muslin to the inside through the frame opening; press.

Step 7. Topstitch around frame opening ¼" from edge and ½" from first stitching line along top edge of center opening only, as shown in Figure 5.

Figure 5

Step 8. Zigzag-stitch along the top edge of the stitched frame and along one edge of the E square to finish edges.

Step 9. Place the E square right sides together with the pieced frame and stitch around sides and across bottom, leaving top zigzagged edges unstitched; turn right side out and press.

Step 10. Turn the top edges of each piece of fabric ¼" to the inside; press and topstitch each piece ⅛" from edge, leaving top edge open. Topstitch side and bottom edges of frame ⅛" from edge.

Step 11. To form photo pocket, topstitch ½" from the inside-opening stitching, connecting with previously stitched line as shown in Figure 6.

Figure 6

Step 12. Cut grosgrain ribbon to make two same-size lengths; fold ends of each piece under 1" to form loops.

Step 13. Pin ribbon pieces over the top of the frame ⅛" from side edges as shown in Figure 7.

Figure 7

Step 14. Sew a button to each pinned piece of ribbon ¼" from bottom folded edge to secure loop ends, again referring to Figure 7.

Step 15. Place clear plastic in frame opening and place photo behind plastic.

COMPLETING THE BEAR

Step 1. Transfer details to bear face using pattern given and a light lead pencil.

Step 2. Using 1 strand black pearl cotton, satin-stitch nose, straight-stitch muzzle lines and add French knots for eyes, wrapping thread around the needle three times.

Step 3. Stack the bear pieces together in pairs; blanket-stitch around edges of pieces to join them, using 2 strands bright blue embroidery floss, stuffing each piece with polyester fiberfill before finishing stitching.

Step 4. Hand-stitch legs and arms to back of body referring to pattern for placement.

Step 5. Wrap pink check ribbon around bear's neck and tie into a bow in the front; trim bow ends even.

Step 6. Sew bear to bottom right corner of frame to finish.

HANGING ROD

Step 1. Drill holes ¾" from each end of the wooden dowel.

Step 2. Insert dowel through ribbon loops.

Step 3. Insert rickrack ends through holes in the dowel and knot ends to secure. ●

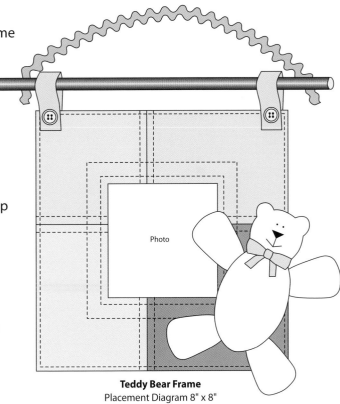

Teddy Bear Frame
Placement Diagram 8" x 8"

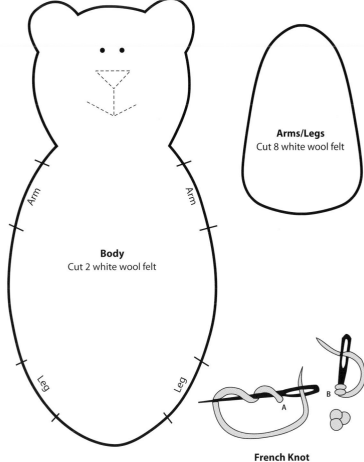

Arms/Legs
Cut 8 white wool felt

Body
Cut 2 white wool felt

Arm

Arm

Leg

Leg

French Knot

Adorable Baby Sets

Baby nurseries are so popular today. Planned with a fun theme, they provide the perfect place to take care of that irresistible baby.

Baby Steps Duo

Designs by Jill Reber

Soft textured fabrics make a cuddly baby quilt and burp cloth.

PROJECT SPECIFICATIONS

Skill Level: Beginner
Quilt Size: 40" x 56"
Burp Cloth Size: 18" x 9½"
Block Size: 8" x 8"
Number of Blocks: 24

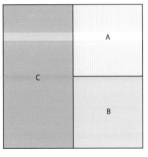

Baby Steps
8" x 8" Block
Make 12

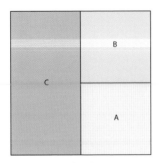

Reversed Baby Steps
8" x 8" Block
Make 12

FABRIC Measurements based on 42" usable width except as noted.	#STRIPS & PIECES	CUT	#PIECES	SUBCUT
½ yard 60"-wide green Minkee	2 1	4½" x 60" 3" x 60"	24 2	4½" B squares 3" x 11" G strips
½ yard yellow chenille	3	4½" x 42"	24	4½" A squares
1⅛ yards blue flannel	3 1	8½" x 42" 10" x 43"	24 2	4½" C rectangles 18" F rectangles
1 yard coordinating plaid	2 3 5	4½" x 32½" D 4½" x 42" E 2¼" x 42" binding		
Backing		46" x 62"		

SUPPLIES

- Batting 46" x 62" and 18" x 10"
- Neutral color all-purpose thread
- Quilting thread
- Green, blue and yellow pearl cotton
- Basic sewing tools and supplies

COMPLETING THE BLOCKS

Step 1. Sew an A square to a B square to make an A-B unit; press seams toward B. Repeat to make 24 A-B units.

Step 2. To make one Baby Steps block, sew an A-B unit to C referring to the block drawing; press seams toward C. Repeat to make 12 Baby Steps blocks.

Step 3. Repeat Step 2, turning the A-B units referring to the block drawing to make 12 Reversed Baby Steps blocks.

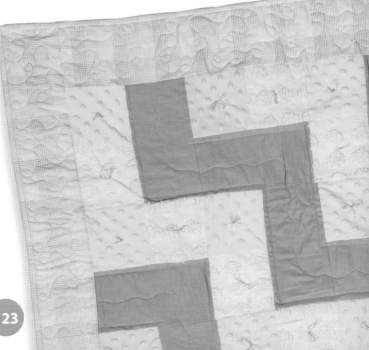

QUILT

COMPLETING THE QUILT

Step 1. Join two Baby Steps and two Reversed Baby Steps blocks to make an X row referring to Figure 1; press seams toward Baby Steps blocks. Repeat to make three X rows.

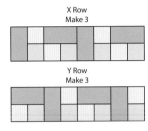

X Row
Make 3

Y Row
Make 3

Figure 1

Step 2. Join two Baby Steps and two Reversed Baby Steps block to make a Y row, again referring to Figure 1; press seams toward Baby Steps blocks. Repeat to make three Y rows.

Step 3. Join the X and Y rows referring to the Placement Diagram for positioning; press seams in one direction.

Step 4. Sew a D strip to the top and bottom of the pieced center; press seams toward D strips.

Step 5. Join the E strips on short ends to make one long strip; press seams open. Subcut strip into two 56½" E strips.

Step 6. Sew an E strip to opposite long sides of the pieced center to complete the pieced top.

Step 7. Finish the quilt referring to the Finishing Instructions on page 173. *Note: The quilt shown was tied with square knots in the center of each A and B square using 2 strands each yellow, green and blue pearl cotton and machine quilted in the C pieces and ditch of seams.*

BURP CLOTH

COMPLETING THE BURP CLOTH

Step 1. Layer the two F rectangles right sides together with the 18" x 10" batting rectangle on top; sew along the two 18" sides.

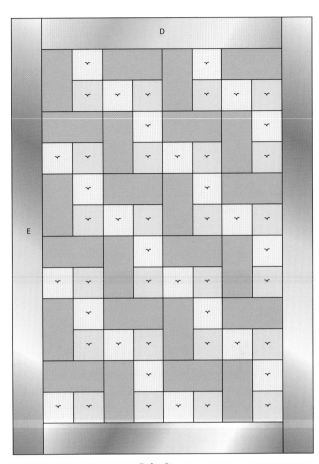

Baby Steps
Placement Diagram 40" x 56"

Step 2. Turn right side out; press seamed edges flat.

Step 3. Quilt as desired.

Step 4. Center and pin a G strip right sides together to each end of the quilted F pieces; stitch using a ½" seam allowance.

Figure 2

Step 5. Press the G strip up; fold short ends of G to the wrong side and fold long side under ¼" as shown in Figure 2. Fold over to the opposite side of F and topstitch folded edges in place as shown in Figure 3 to finish. ●

Figure 3

Burp Cloth
Placement Diagram 18" x 9½"

Animal Fun

Designs by Sandra L. Hatch

Look for a fun animal print to make a simple quilt with matching bag.

Animal Fun
8" x 8" Block
Make 12

PROJECT SPECIFICATIONS

Skill Level: Beginner
Quilt Size: 43" x 53"
Tote Bag Size: 15" x 12"
Block Size: 8" x 8"
Number of Blocks: 12

PROJECT NOTES

If you have a sewing machine with built-in embroidery designs, you could use the designs to make the block centers and the quilt corners. This quilt uses a Winnie the Pooh design that is built into the Brother Innovis-D sewing machine. It is a perfect coordinate to the Disney-design fabrics used in the quilt.

QUILT

COMPLETING THE BLOCKS

Step 1. Sew a B strip to a C strip to a D strip with right sides together along the length; press seams in one direction. Repeat to make three strip sets.

Step 2. Sew an E strip to each side of two B-C-D strip sets to make two B-C-D-E strip sets; press seams in one direction.

Step 3. Subcut the strip sets into (24) 1½" B-C-D units and (38) 1½" B-C-D-E units as shown in Figure 1.

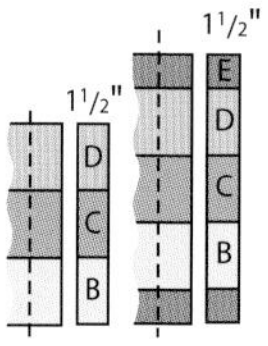

1½"   1½"

Figure 1

FABRIC FOR QUILT Measurements based on 42" usable fabric width.		#STRIPS & PIECES	CUT	#PIECES	SUBCUT
	¼ yard white tonal	4	4½" x 4½" M		
	⅓ yard yellow tonal	3	2½" x 42" B		
	⅓ yard lavender tonal	3	2½" x 42" C		
	½ yard melon tonal	4	1½" x 42" E		
		2	2½" x 42"	20	2½" G squares
				4	1½" E squares
	½ yard light green tonal	3	2½" x 42" D		
		2	1" x 35½" J		
		3	1" x 42" I		
	1⅛ yards coordinating stripe	7	2½" x 42"	31	8½" F pieces
				18	1½" H pieces
		5	2¼" x 42" binding		
	1⅛ yards animal print	2	4½" x 35½" L		
		2	4½" x 45½" K along length		
		12	6½" x 6½" A with motif centered		
Backing			49" x 59"		

SUPPLIES

- Batting 49" x 59"
- Neutral color all-purpose thread
- Quilting thread
- Machine-embroidery thread as desired
- Basic sewing tools and supplies

Step 4. To complete one Animal Fun block, sew a B-C-D unit to opposite sides of A referring to the block drawing for positioning; press seams toward A.

©Disney

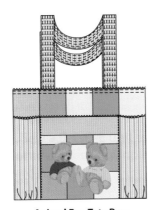

Animal Fun Tote Bag
Placement Diagram 15" x 12"

Step 15. Pull gathering stitches along bottom edges to pull up the bottom of the B and D pieces to fit as pinned.

Step 16. Stitch along seams between D and the B-C unit matching to seams of the A unit as shown in Figure 11 to attach pocket unit to the A unit; secure stitching at the top edge.

Figure 11

Step 17. Machine-baste the pocket unit to the A unit to hold in place to complete the bag front. *Note: The D pocket area will not be flat; the B-C pocket area will be almost flat.*

Step 18. Join the bag front with the remaining A unit (bag back) along one 12½" edge as shown in Figure 12; press seam open.

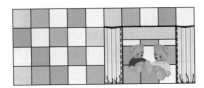

Figure 12

Step 19. Machine-baste the 30½" length rickrack along the top edge of the bag unit.

MAKING THE HANDLES

Step 1. Fold one long edge of each handle strip ¼" to the wrong side and press.

Step 2. Fold over opposite long raw edge of each strip to the center as shown in Figure 13 and press; fold the pressed ¼" edge on top of the raw edge of strip and press.

Figure 13   **Figure 14**

Step 3. Open the pressed edges of each strip and insert a 1½"-wide batting strip, aligning batting strip with pressed lines as shown in Figure 14.

Step 4. Refold pressed edges over the batting, first folding over the raw edges, then overlapping with the folded edge; press to make 1½"-wide strips.

Step 5. Stitch along folded-over edge along center of strips as shown in Figure 15. Stitch ¼" lines on each side as shown in Figure 16.

Figure 15   **Figure 16**

Step 6. Square up ends of each strip to complete handles.

ATTACHING THE HANDLES

Step 1. Fold the quilted bag top in half along the width and lay on a flat surface.

Step 2. Measure in 3¾" from the raw edge and pin the right side of one end of one handle to the top right side edge of the bag as shown in Figure 17.

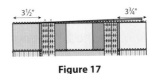

Figure 17

Step 3. Measure in 3½" from the folded edge and pin the opposite end of the same handle right sides together with bag top edge referring to Figure 17. **Note:** *The right side of the handle strip is the side without the overlapped edge.*

Step 4. Turn folded bag top over, align and pin the second handle even with the ends of the handle pinned in step 2 as shown in Figure 18.

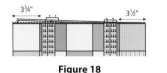

Figure 18

Figure 19

Step 5. Machine-stitch over ends of handles several times to secure in place as shown in Figure 19.

COMPLETING THE BAG

Step 1. Place lining piece right sides together with quilted top. Stitch across top edge of bag, stitching over handle ends.

Step 2. Press seam toward lining and topstitch close to seam on lining side as shown in Figure 20.

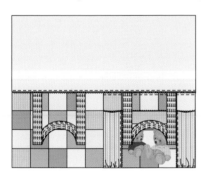

Figure 20

Step 3. Fold bag top and lining sections with right sides together as shown in Figure 21. Starting at the bag bottom corner, stitch all around bag top and lining, leaving a 6" opening in the bottom edge of the lining as shown in Figure 22.

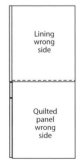

Figure 21

Figure 22

Step 4. Trim corners of bag top and lining, and trim batting close to seam at top side edge and along bottom corners to reduce bulk.

Step 5. Turn right side out through opening in lining, making sure corners are completely turned.

Step 6. Press seam inside at lining opening edges and machine-stitch opening closed close to edges as shown in Figure 23.

Figure 23

Step 7. Before inserting lining inside bag, press side seam of bag to help make bag lie flat at sides when complete.

Step 8. Insert lining inside bag. Press lining to the inside at the top edge of the bag. Insert iron inside bag and press lining flat as far inside as the iron will slide. Hold the top side of the bag and insert your hand inside the bag to the corners to be sure lining is completely inside and aligned at corners.

Step 9. Topstitch along top edge of bag ¼"–⅜" from edge using thread to match fabrics or clear nylon in the top of the machine and all-purpose thread in the bobbin. ●

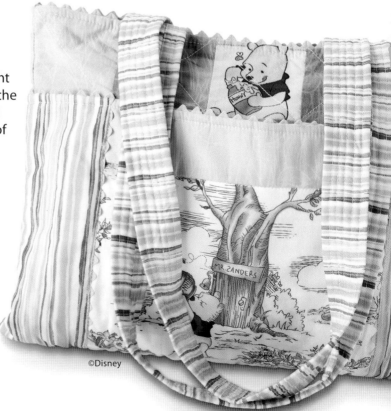

©Disney

Flower Fancies

Designs by Connie Kauffman

Use luxurious Minkee fabric without batting to make a soft baby blanket with a matching bumper pad.

PROJECT SPECIFICATIONS

Skill Level: Intermediate
Quilt Size: 42" x 42"
Bumper Size: 156" x 9"
Block Size: 6" x 6"
Number of Blocks: 25 for quilt, 6 for bumper pad

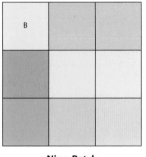

Nine-Patch
6" x 6" Block
Make 13

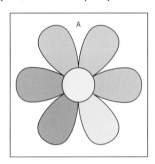

Flower
6" x 6" Block
Make 12

QUILT

COMPLETING THE NINE-PATCH BLOCKS

Step 1. Join the B squares in sets of three; press seams in one direction. Repeat to make 39 B units.

Step 2. To make one Nine-Patch block, join three B units with seams in rows in opposite directions. Press seams in one direction. Repeat to make 13 Nine-Patch blocks.

FABRIC Measurements based on 43" usable fabric width except as noted.	#STRIPS & PIECES	CUT	#PIECES	SUBCUT
22—2½" x 43" assorted strips	117 20 2	2½" B squares total 9" H 28½" I Appliqué pieces as per pattern		
⅓ yard large pink floral	1	7" x 43"	4	9½" G rectangles
⅓ yard large lilac floral	1	7" x 43"	4	9½" G rectangles
⅓ yard large blue floral	1	7" x 43"	4	9½" G rectangles
¾ yard white tonal	2 1	6½" x 43" 9½" x 43"	12 6	6½" A squares 7" E rectangles
⅞ yard aqua floral	2 2	6½" x 30½" C 6½" x 42½" D		
1 yard multicolored lengthwise stripe	5 2	2¼" x 43" binding 9½" x 43"	12	3¾" F strips
1⅛ yards pink floral	4	9½" x 43" J		
1⅜ yards yellow 60"-wide Minkee		46" x 46" quilt backing Appliqué pieces as per pattern		

SUPPLIES

- Thick batting 9½" x 156½"
- Neutral color and yellow all-purpose thread
- Quilting thread
- 1⅝ yards 12"-wide fusible web
- 1½ yards fabric stabilizer
- Appliqué pressing sheet
- Basic sewing tools and supplies

COMPLETING THE FLOWER BLOCKS

Step 1. Trace petal and center shapes onto the paper side of the fusible web as directed on patterns; cut out leaving a margin around each one.

Step 2. Fuse shapes to the wrong sides of fabrics as directed on patterns; cut out shapes on traced lines. Remove paper backing.

Step 3. Fold and crease each A square to mark the centers.

Step 4. Trace the appliqué motif onto a piece of paper; place the traced shape under the appliqué pressing sheet. Arrange shapes in place on the pressing sheet to complete one flower motif, overlapping petals and covering with the flower center; fuse in place. Repeat to make 22 flower motifs; set aside four motifs for borders and six for bumper pad.

Step 5. Arrange and fuse one flower motif on the center of each A square.

Step 6. Cut (22) 6" x 6" squares fabric stabilizer; set aside four squares for borders and six for bumper pad. Pin a square to the wrong side of each fused A square.

Step 7. Using a narrow machine buttonhole stitch and yellow thread, stitch around each fused shape to complete the blocks. Remove fabric stabilizer.

COMPLETING THE QUILT

Step 1. Join three Nine-Patch blocks with two Flower blocks to make an X row as shown in Figure 1; press seams toward Flower blocks. Repeat to make three X rows.

Step 2. Join three Flower blocks with two Nine-Patch blocks to make a Y row, again referring to Figure 1; press seams toward Flower blocks. Repeat to make two Y rows.

Step 3. Join the rows referring to the Placement Diagram to complete the pieced center; press seams in one direction.

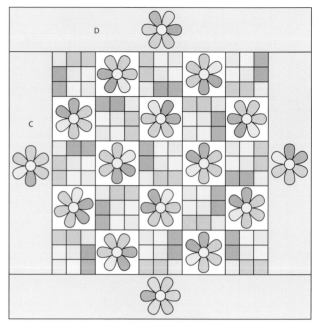

Flower Fancies Quilt
Placement Diagram 42" x 42"

Step 4. Fold each C and D strip and crease to mark the centers; center and fuse a flower motif on each crease and appliqué in place as in Steps 6 and 7 of Completing the Flower Blocks.

Step 5. Sew a C strip to opposite sides and D strips to the top and bottom of the pieced center to complete the pieced top; press seams toward C and D strips.

Step 6. Finish the quilt referring to the Finishing Instructions on page 173.

BUMPER PAD

COMPLETING THE BUMPER TOP

Step 1. Complete six appliquéd E rectangles as in Completing the Flower Blocks.

Step 2. Sew an F strip to opposite sides of each appliqué E rectangle as shown in Figure 2; press seams toward F.

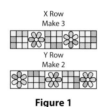

X Row
Make 3

Y Row
Make 2

Figure 1

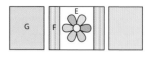

Figure 2

Step 3. Sew G to the F sides of each E-F unit, again referring to Figure 2; press seams toward G. Repeat to make six E-F-G units.

Step 4. Join the E-F-G units to complete the bumper pad top as shown in Figure 3; press seams in one direction.

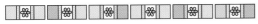
Figure 3

COMPLETING THE BUMPER PAD

Step 1. Fold each short end of the H and I strips ¼" to the wrong side; press.

Step 2. Fold each H and I strip wrong sides together along length and press to crease the center. Unfold and press each side to the center; fold along crease again and stitch only the H strips as shown in Figure 4. Set aside I strips for ends.

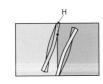

Figure 4   **Figure 5**

Step 3. Pin two H ties at the top and bottom of each E-F-G unit intersection as shown in Figure 5; baste to hold in place.

Step 4. Join the J pieces on short ends to make one long strip; press seams open. Trim to 156½" long for backing.

Step 5. Lay the batting on a flat surface; layer the pieced bumper top right side up and the backing right sides together with the top; pin the layers together along one long side.

Step 6. Stitch through all layers along one long edge using a ¼" seam allowance. *Note: It is helpful to use a walking foot for the stitching for this and remaining steps.*

Step 7. Fold the backing to the wrong side to enclose batting; press and pin raw edges of the remaining long side and both ends together as shown in Figure 6. Baste to hold.

Figure 6   **Figure 7**

Step 8. Stitch in the ditch of each seam through all layers as shown in Figure 7.

Step 9. Join the binding strips on short ends to make one long strip; press seams open.

Step 10. Fold and press binding strips as for H and I strips in Steps 1 and 2.

Step 11. Enclose raw edges of the stitched bumper pad with the binding and stitch close to pressed edges as shown in Figure 8.

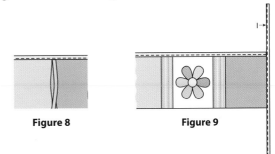

Figure 8   **Figure 9**

Step 12. Repeat Step 11 with I strips on each raw end to complete the bumper pad as shown in Figure 9. ●

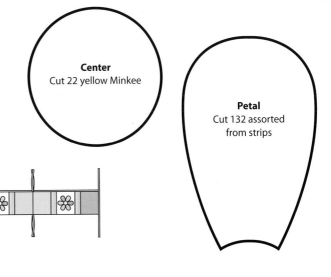

Center
Cut 22 yellow Minkee

Petal
Cut 132 assorted from strips

Flower Fancies Bumper Pad
Placement Diagram 156" x 9"

Nursery Quilt & Runner

Designs by Jill Reber

Showcase a novelty print in the center of a block to add interest to this baby quilt with matching runner.

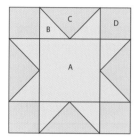

Star
8" x 8" Block
Make 4 for quilt
Make 1 for runner

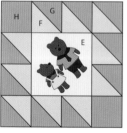

Diagonal Novelty
8" x 8" Block
Make 9

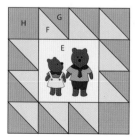

Straight Novelty
8" x 8" Block
Make 2

PROJECT SPECIFICATIONS

Skill Level: Beginner
Quilt Size: 42⅛" x 42⅛"
Runner Size: 32" x 16"
Block Size: 8" x 8"
Number of Blocks: 13 for quilt; 3 for runner

COMPLETING THE STAR BLOCKS

Step 1. Mark a diagonal line from corner to corner on the wrong side of each B square.

Step 2. Place a B square right sides together on one end of C and stitch on the marked line as shown in Figure 1; trim seam to ¼" and press seam toward B. Repeat on the remaining end of C as shown in Figure 2 to complete one B-C unit. Repeat to complete 20 units.

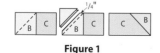

Figure 1

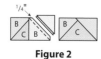

Figure 2

FABRIC Measurements based on 43" usable fabric width.	#STRIPS & PIECES	CUT	#PIECES	SUBCUT
½ yard focus fabric or enough to cut 11 E squares	9	Fussy-cut 4½" E squares with motif centered diagonally		
	2	4½" E squares with motif centered straight		
⅝ yard green tonal stripe	4	2⅞" x 43"	55	2⅞" G squares
	2	2½" x 43"	22	2½" H squares
⅝ yard gold tonal	3	2½" x 43"	40	2½" B squares
	1	4½" x 43"	5	4½" A squares
1¼ yards blue tonal	2	4½" x 43"	20	2½" C rectangles
	2	2½" x 43"	20	2½" D squares
	4	2⅞" x 43"	55	2⅞" F squares
	1	12⅝" x 43"	2	12⅝" squares; cut on both diagonals to make 8 I triangles
			2	6½" squares; cut in half on 1 diagonal to make 4 J triangles
1⅜ yards blue-and-white diagonal plaid	2	4½" x 34⅝" K		
	2	4½" x 43⅝" L		
	2	4½" x 43	2	4½" x 32½" N
	7	2¼" x 43" binding	2	4½" x 8½" M
Backing		48" x 48"		

SUPPLIES

- Batting 48" x 48"
- Neutral color all-purpose thread
- Quilting thread
- Basic sewing tools and supplies

Step 3. To complete one Star block, sew a B-C unit to opposite sides of A to complete the center row as shown in Figure 3; press seams toward A.

Figure 3

Step 4. Sew D to each end of two B-C units as shown in Figure 4 to complete the top and bottom rows; press seams toward D.

Figure 4

Step 5. Sew the top and bottom rows to the center row referring to the block drawing for positioning; press seams away from the center row.

Step 6. Repeat Steps 3–5 to complete five Star blocks.

COMPLETING THE NOVELTY BLOCKS
Step 1. Mark a diagonal line from corner to corner on the wrong side of each G square.

Step 2. Place an F square right sides together with G and stitch ¼" on each side of the marked line as shown in Figure 5. Cut the stitched unit apart on the marked line and press open with seams toward G, again referring to Figure 5 to make two F-G units. Repeat with all F and G squares to complete 110 F-G units.

Figure 5

Step 3. To complete one Diagonal Novelty block, join two F-G units as shown in Figure 6 to make an F-G side row; press seam in one direction. Repeat to make two F-G side rows.

Figure 6

Step 4. Sew an F-G side row to opposite sides of a diagonal E to make the center row as shown in Figure 7; press seams toward E.

Figure 7

Step 5. Join three F-G units with H to complete the top row as shown in Figure 8; press seams toward H. Repeat to make the bottom row.

Figure 8

Step 6. Sew the top and bottom rows to the center row to complete one Diagonal Novelty block referring to the block drawing; press seams toward the center row.

Step 7. Repeat Steps 3–6 to complete nine Diagonal Novelty blocks.

Step 8. Repeat Steps 3–6 with straight E squares to make two Straight Novelty blocks.

QUILT

COMPLETING THE QUILT

Step 1. Arrange and join four Star and nine Diagonal Novelty blocks in diagonal rows with I and J referring to Figure 9; press seams in one direction and toward I and J.

Figure 9

Step 2. Join the rows to complete the pieced center; press seams in one direction.

Step 3. Sew a K strip to the top and bottom, and L strips to opposite sides of the pieced center to complete the pieced top; press seams toward K and L strips.

Step 4. Finish the quilt referring to the Finishing Instructions on page 173.

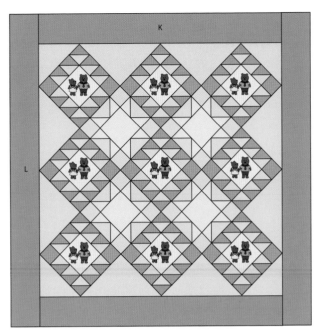

Nursery Quilt
Placement Diagram 42⅛" x 42⅛"

RUNNER

COMPLETING THE RUNNER

Step 1. Sew a Star block between two Straight Novelty blocks to complete the pieced center; press seams toward the Star block.

Step 2. Sew M to opposite short ends and N to opposite long sides of the pieced center to complete the pieced top.

Step 3. Finish the runner referring to the Finishing Instructions on page 173. ●

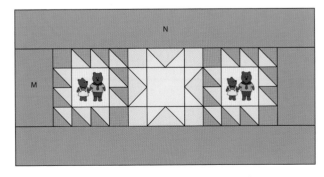

Nursery Runner
Placement Diagram 32" x 16"

Ducks Around the World

Designs by Barbara Clayton

Appliquéd ducks combine with a Trip Around the World center in this quilt with matching burp cloth.

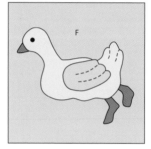

Mother Duck
5" x 5" Block
Make 4

Baby Duck
5" x 5" Block
Make 12

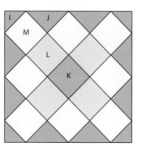

Corner
7" x 7" Block
Make 4

PROJECT SPECIFICATIONS

Skill Level: Advanced
Quilt Size: 44" x 44" without prairie points
Burp Cloth Size: 9" x 22"
Block Size: 5" x 5" and 7" x 7"
Number of Blocks: 16 and 4

QUILT

COMPLETING THE DUCK BLOCKS

Step 1. Trace the large duck pattern pieces on the paper side of the freezer paper referring to the patterns for number to cut.

Step 2. Cut out the freezer-paper patterns on the traced lines.

Step 3. Press the waxy side of the freezer-paper patterns onto the back side of fabrics as directed on patterns for color.

FABRIC FOR QUILT Measurements based on 42" usable fabric width.	#STRIPS & PIECES	CUT	#PIECES	SUBCUT
Scrap orange tonal		Appliqué pieces as per patterns		
Fat quarter medium yellow tonal		Appliqué pieces as per patterns		
Fat quarter light yellow tonal		Appliqué pieces as per patterns		
⅝ yard green-white gingham	3	5½" x 42"	16	5½" F squares
⅞ yard bright yellow print	4	2½" x 42"	56	2½" C squares
	1	8⅜" x 42"	3	8⅜" squares; cut on both diagonals to make 12 H1 triangles
	1	4⅜" x 42"	4	4⅜" squares; cut in half on 1 diagonal to make 8 G1 triangles
		L pieces as per template		
1 yard yellow/white stripe	4	2½" x 42"	56	2½" B squares
	1	8⅜" x 42"	3	8⅜" squares; cut on both diagonals to make 12 H2 triangles
	1	4⅜" x 42"	4	4⅜" squares; cut in half on 1 diagonal to make 8 G2 triangles
		M pieces as per template		

FABRIC FOR QUILT Measurements based on 42" usable fabric width.	#STRIPS & PIECES	CUT	#PIECES	SUBCUT
▨ 1⅔ yards medium green solid	4	2½" x 42"	57	2½" A squares
	7	3½" x 42"	84	3½" P squares
	2	1½" x 26½" D		
	2	1½" x 28½" E		
	5	1½" x 42" N/O		
		I, J and K pieces as per templates		
Backing		48" x 48"		

SUPPLIES

- Batting 51" x 51"
- All-purpose thread to match fabrics
- Green quilting thread
- Clear nylon thread
- Black embroidery floss
- Plain paper
- Freezer paper
- Fabric glue stick
- Basic sewing tools and supplies

Step 4. Cut out each shape adding ¼" all around for turn-under seam allowance; clip curves, points and indentations carefully almost to the paper pattern.

Step 5. Using a fabric glue stick, glue the ¼" excess fabric over the edge and to the back of the freezer paper; glue all the way around each appliqué.

Step 6. Fold each F square on both diagonals and crease to mark the center.

Step 7. Hand-stitch shapes in place in numerical order using thread to match fabrics. *Note: If you prefer to machine-appliqué, lower your feed dogs, use a darning foot and slowly machine-stitch around each shape using clear nylon thread and a narrow blind-hem stitch.*

Step 8. Cut a slit behind each appliqué shape; trim away the background to ¼" from the edge of the stitching inside appliqués. Use a sponge or wet cloth to wet the back of each appliqué to loosen glue; remove freezer-paper shapes. Set aside blocks and let dry.

Step 9. Hand-stitch the eye on each duck using 1 strand black embroidery floss. Set aside blocks.

COMPLETING THE CORNER BLOCKS

Step 1. Join K, L and M squares in diagonal rows referring to Figure 1; press seams in adjoining rows in opposite directions.

Figure 1

Step 2. Add I and J triangles to ends of rows, again referring to Figure 1; press seams toward I and J.

Step 3. Join the rows as arranged to complete one Corner block; press seams in one direction.

Step 4. Repeat Steps 1–3 to complete four Corner blocks.

COMPLETING THE QUILT CENTER

Step 1. Join five A and four each B and C squares to make an X row as shown in Figure 2; press seams away from B. Repeat to make five X rows.

Step 2. Join four each A and C, and five B squares to make a Y row, again referring to Figure 2; press seams away from B. Repeat to make four Y rows.

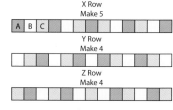

Figure 2

Step 3. Join four each A and B, and five C squares to make a Z row, again referring to Figure 2; press seams away from B. Repeat to make four Z rows.

Step 4. Join the rows in the following order to complete the quilt center: X, Y, Z, X, Y, Z, X, Z, Y, X, Z, Y and X. Press seams in one direction.

COMPLETING THE QUILT

Step 1. Sew a D strip to opposite sides and E strips to the top and bottom of the pieced center; press seams toward D and E strips.

Step 2. Sew H1 and H2 to opposite sides of a Baby Duck block as shown in Figure 3; press seams toward H. Repeat to make two H/Duck units.

Figure 3   **Figure 4**

Step 3. Sew H2 to one side and G1 and G2 to two adjacent sides of a Mother Duck block to make a corner unit as shown in Figure 4; repeat with G1, G2 and H1 and a Baby Duck block to make a reversed corner unit, again referring to Figure 4. Press seams toward H and G.

Step 4. Join the H/Duck units with the G-H/Duck units to complete a side strip as shown in Figure 5; press seams in one direction. Repeat to make four side strips.

Figure 5

Step 5. Sew a side strip to opposite sides of the pieced center referring to the Placement Diagram for positioning of strips; press seams toward D strips.

Step 6. Sew a Corner block to each end of each remaining side strip; press seams toward side strips.

Step 7. Sew a side/Corner block strip to the top and bottom of the pieced center, again referring to the Placement Diagram; press seams toward E strips.

Step 8. Join N/O strips on short ends to make one long strip; press seams open. Subcut strip into two 42½" N strips and two 44½" O strips.

Step 9. Sew N strips to opposite sides and O strips to the top and bottom of the pieced center; press seams toward N and O strips.

Step 10. Fold each P square in half on one diagonal and in half again to form a folded triangle or prairie point as shown in Figure 6; press to hold.

Figure 6

Ducks Around the World
Placement Diagram 44" x 44"
without prairie points

Step 11. Pin the raw edges of 21 folded triangles to each side of the pieced top, equally spacing by overlapping one inside the other about 1½" as shown in Figure 7; machine-baste to hold in place.

Figure 7

Step 12. Lay the batting square on a flat surface; lay the backing square on top of the batting with right side up and pin to the batting.

Step 13. Pin the completed quilt top right sides together with the backing with prairie points tucked inside; stitch all around, leaving an 8" opening on one side.

Step 14. Trim the corners and excess batting and backing; turn right side out through the opening, pulling the prairie points outward.

Step 15. Turn the opening edges ¼" to the inside and hand-stitch closed.

FABRIC FOR BURP CLOTH Measurements based on 42" usable fabric width.	#STRIPS & PIECES	CUT	#PIECES	SUBCUT
Scraps orange and light and medium yellow tonals		Appliqué pieces as per patterns		
⅛ yard bright yellow print	2	1½" x 42"	2 2	20½" B 9½" C
¼ yard green-white gingham	2	2¼" x 42" binding		
⅓ yard light green flannel	1	7½" x 42"	1	20½" A rectangle
Backing		13" x 26"		

Step 16. Machine-quilt in the ditch of all seams using clear nylon thread and a walking foot. Hand-quilt around all appliquéd parts of the ducks and along the quilting lines in the wings and tail feathers and ¼" from all seam lines using green quilting thread to finish.

BURP CLOTH

COMPLETING THE BURP CLOTH

Step 1. Trace the small mother and baby duck shapes onto the paper side of the fusible web as directed on patterns; cut out shapes, leaving a margin around each one.

Step 2. Fuse shapes to the wrong side of fabric scraps as directed on patterns for color; cut out shapes on traced lines. Remove paper backing.

Step 3. Arrange and fuse the mother and baby duck pieces in numerical order ¾" from the bottom edge and 1" from each side edge of A as shown in Figure 8.

Figure 8

Step 4. Cut a 6" x 7" piece of fabric stabilizer; pin to the wrong side of A under the fused duck shapes.

Step 5. Using thread to match fabrics and a narrow machine zigzag stitch, sew around each fused shape.

SUPPLIES

- Batting 13" x 26"
- All-purpose thread to match fabrics
- Green quilting thread
- Black embroidery floss
- ⅛ yard 18"-wide fusible web
- ¼ yard fabric stabilizer
- Water-erasable marker
- Basic sewing tools and supplies

Step 6. Add French knots for eyes using 2 strands black embroidery floss.

Step 7. Draw diagonal lines spaced 1¼" apart on A using the water-erasable marker.

Step 8. Sew B strips to opposite long sides and C strips to opposite short ends of A; press seams toward B and C strips.

Step 9. Finish the burp cloth referring to the Finishing Instructions on page 173, machine-quilting on marked lines. Remove marked lines using a dampened sponge or cloth. ●

Ducks Burp Cloth
Placement Diagram 9" x 22"

I
Cut 16
medium
green solid

J
Cut 32 medium
green solid

K/L/M
Cut 4 medium green
solid (K), 16 bright
yellow print (L) & 32
yellow/white stripe (M)

orange
1
medium
yellow
4
light yellow
3
orange
2
orange

Small Mother Duck
Complete 1 of this motif.

orange
1
5
medium
yellow
4
light yellow
3
orange
2
orange

Small Baby Duck
Complete 1 of this motif.

orange
1
5
medium
yellow
4
light yellow
Center
3
orange
2
orange

Large Baby Duck
Complete 12 of this motif.

orange
1
light yellow
4
Center
5
medium
yellow
3
orange
2
orange

Large Mother Duck
Complete 4 of this motif.

Bright & Charming Baby

Designs by Connie Kauffman

Use lively charm square prints to make this nursery set.

PROJECT SPECIFICATIONS

Skill Level: Intermediate
Quilt Size: 30" x 34"
Dust Ruffle: 78" x 54"
Valance: 75½" x 12"

QUILT

COMPLETING THE QUILT

Step 1. Arrange and join the A squares in five rows of four squares each; press seams in adjoining rows in opposite direction.

Step 2. Join the rows to complete the pieced center.

Step 3. Sew B strips to opposite sides and C strips to the top and bottom of the pieced center; press seams toward B and C strips.

Step 4. Join seven D squares with six F squares, alternating D and F pieces; press seams in one direction. Repeat to make two D-F strips; sew a strip to opposite long sides of the pieced center. Press seams toward B strips.

Step 5. Join five F squares with six D squares and two E squares to make a D-E-F strip as shown in Figure 1; press seams in one direction and toward E. Repeat to make two D-E-F strips.

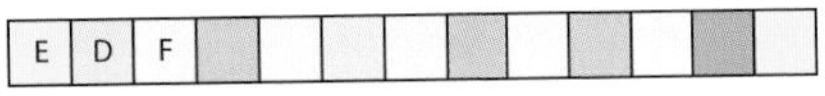

| E | D | F | | | | | | | | | | |

Figure 1

FABRIC Measurements based on 42" usable fabric width.	#STRIPS & PIECES	CUT	#PIECES	SUBCUT
36— 5" A squares coordinating prints	4	2½" D squares from each of 16 of the squares		
⅓ yard white/ strawberry print	1	9" x 16½" I		
⅓ yard pink/ strawberry print	1	9" x 16½" I		
⅓ yard white floral	2	9" x 16½" J		
⅓ yard blue floral	1	9" x 16½" I		
½ yard white-with-dots	5	2½" x 42"	58 4	2½" F squares 2¾" H rectangles
	1	9" x 16½" I		
⅔ yard light green print	2	2½" x 23" B		
	2	2¼" x 22½" C		
	1	9" x 16½" I		
	3	2½" x 42" P		
	2	2½" x 27" Q		
2⅛ yards dark green print	4	2¼" x 42" binding		
	4	2½" x 30½" G		
	2	8½" x 51" N along the length		
	1	9" x 16½" I along the length		
	2	8½" x 27" O along the length		
3 yards yellow stripe: cut all along length of fabric	1	26½" x 50½" K strip		
	2	8½" x 51" L strips		
	2	8½" x 27" M strips		
	1	9" x 16½" I piece		
	4	2½" x 2½" E squares		
Backing		36" x 40"		

SUPPLIES

- Batting 36" x 40"
- Neutral color all-purpose thread
- Quilting thread
- Basic sewing tools and supplies

Step 6. Sew a D-E-F strip to the top and bottom of the pieced center; press seams toward C strips.

Step 7. Sew a G strip to opposite long sides and then to the top and bottom of the pieced center; press seams toward G strips.

Step 8. Finish the quilt referring to the Finishing Instructions on page 173.

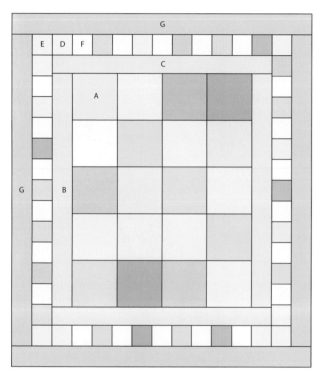

Bright & Charming Baby Quilt
Placement Diagram 30" x 34"

DUST RUFFLE

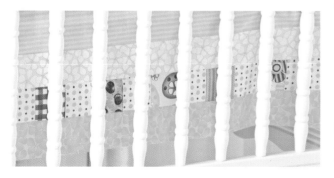

COMPLETING THE DUST RUFFLE

Step 1. Join 12 D and 13 F squares to make a D-F strip; press seams in one direction. Repeat to make two D-F strips.

Step 2. Sew N to one side, and P and L to the remaining side of each D-F strip to make two side panels as shown in Figure 2; press seams away from the D-F strip.

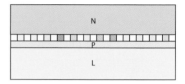

Figure 2

Step 3. Join five F and six D squares and add H to each end to make a D-F-H strip as shown in Figure 3; press seams in one direction. Repeat to make two D-F-H strips.

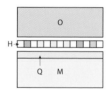

Figure 3

Step 4. Sew O to one side, and Q and M to the remaining side of each D-F-H strip to make two end panels, again referring to Figure 3; press seams away from the D-F-H strip.

Step 5. Zigzag or serge the long edges of L and M pieces on each panel to finish edges.

Step 6. Fold under ¼" along the N and O edges of each panel; press to hold.

Step 7. Fold the N and O pieces to the wrong side to enclose seams as shown in Figure 4; hand-stitch to hold in place.

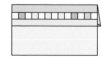

Figure 4

Step 8. Turn under short ends ¼"; press. Turn under again, press and hand-stitch in place to finish edges.

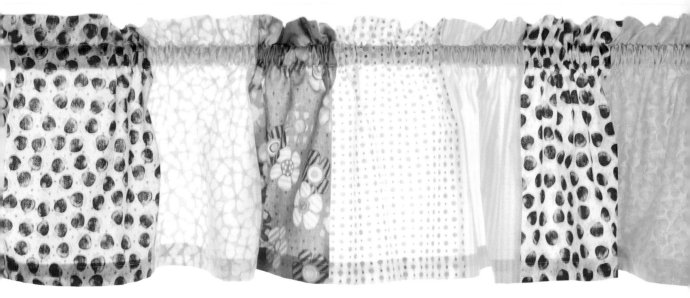

Step 9. Machine-stitch in the ditch of seams of each side and end panel as shown in Figure 5.

Figure 5

Step 10. Center, pin and stitch a side panel on opposite long sides of K as shown in Figure 6. ***Note:*** *There should be ¼" open on each end of K to allow for end panel seams.*

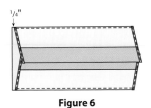

Figure 6

Step 11. Repeat Step 10 with each end panel, folding side panels out of the way of stitching.

Step 12. Zigzag or serge seams to prevent fraying during use and washing.

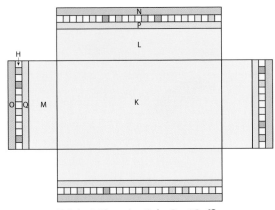

Bright & Charming Baby Dust Ruffle
Placement Diagram 78" x 54"

VALANCE

COMPLETING THE VALANCE

Step 1. Arrange and join the seven I rectangles with a J rectangle at each end; press seams in one direction.

Step 2. Zigzag or serge each seam to prevent fraying during use and washing.

Step 3. Fold in ¼" on each end and press; fold in ¼" again and stitch to hem.

Step 4. Fold the bottom edge to the wrong side ½" and press; fold 1" to the wrong side, press and stitch to hem.

Step 5. Fold the top edge to the inside ¼" and press. Fold 2¾" to the wrong side; press and stitch close to the pressed edge as shown in Figure 7.

Figure 7

Step 6. Mark and stitch a line 1¼" from the stitched line to form casing for hanging rod to finish, again referring to Figure 7. ***Note:*** *If more fullness is desired, cut and add another I rectangle when stitching.* ●

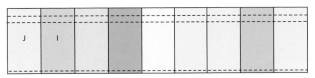

Bright & Charming Baby Valance
Placement Diagram 75½" x 12"

Inch by Inch

Designs by Jennifer Foltz

Make a coordinated set including a crib quilt, bumper pads, organizer and valance using a cute inchworm design.

PROJECT SPECIFICATIONS

Skill Level: Intermediate
Quilt Size: 37½" x 45"
Organizer Size: 27" x 22½"
Bumper Pad Size: 26" x 10" x 1" each piece
Valance Size: 62" x 16" (without tabs)
Block Size: 6" x 6" and 10" x 10"
Number of Blocks: 23 and 9

Worm Body
6" x 6" Block
Make 11 for quilt
Make 2 for nursery organizer

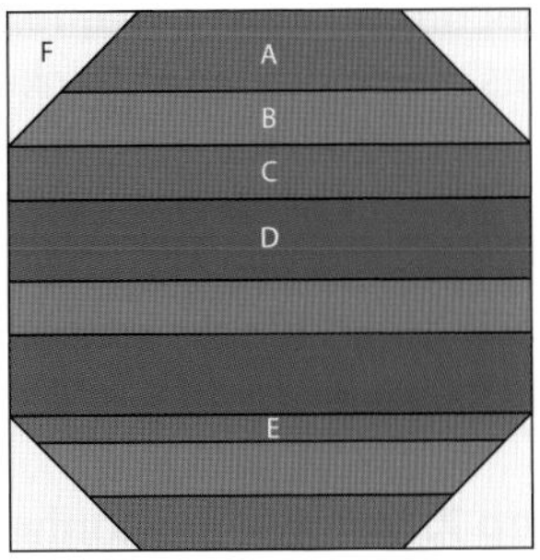

Stripe
10" x 10" Block
Make 9

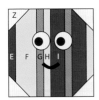

Worm Head
6" x 6" Block
Make 1 for quilt
Make 1 for nursery organizer

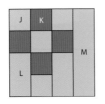

Flower
6" x 6" Block
Make 2 each yellow & orange & 4 green

QUILT

COMPLETING THE WORM BODY BLOCKS

Step 1. Join one A, two D and three each B and C strips with right sides together along length to

FABRIC FOR QUILT Measurements based on 43" usable fabric width.	#STRIPS & PIECES	CUT	#PIECES	SUBCUT
⬛ Scrap black solid		Appliqué pieces as per patterns		
¼ yard orange tonal	2	1" x 43" G		
	1	2" x 43" O		
¼ yard yellow tonal	2	1" x 43" H		
	1	2" x 43" F		
	1	2" x 43" N		
⅓ yard red tonal	1	1" x 43" E		
	2	1½" x 43" I		
	1	3½" x 43 P		
⅜ yard dark aqua tonal	9	1" x 43" B		
½ yard light green tonal	3	2" x 43" J		
	3	2" x 43"	8	6½" M
			16	3½" L
⅞ yard cream tonal	11	2" x 43"	60	2" Z squares
			4	23" R strips
			8	6½" S pieces
			2	29" T strips
			2	39½" U strips
	2	2" x 43" Q Appliqué pieces as per pattern (for eyes)		
1 yard dark green tonal	1	3½" x 35" W		
	1	3½" x 39½" V		
	9	1" x 43" C		
	3	1½" x 43" A		
	1	2" x 43" K		
1⅛ yards dark blue tonal	6	1½" x 43" D		
	1	3½" x 42½" X		
	1	3½" x 38" Y		
	5	2¼" x 43" binding		
Backing		44" x 51"		

Step 7. Join one orange Flower and three Worm Body blocks with one S piece and two P-Q units as shown in Figure 12 to make Row 5; press seams away from blocks.

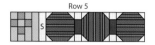

Row 5

Figure 12

Step 8. Sew one P-Q unit to an R strip to make a sashing row as shown in Figure 13; press seams toward R strip. Repeat to make four sashing rows.

Sashing Row
Make 4

R

Figure 13

Step 9. Arrange and join the block rows in numerical order with the sashing rows referring to the Placement Diagram for positioning; press seams toward sashing rows.

Step 10. Sew T strips to the top and bottom and U strips to opposite sides of the pieced center; press seams toward T and U strips.

Step 11. Sew the V, W, X and Y strips to quilt edges in alphabetical order referring to the Placement Diagram for positioning of strips; press seams toward strips.

Step 12. Arrange and fuse the antennae above the Worm Head block referring to the Placement Diagram for positioning. Set aside remaining antenna pieces for the Nursery Organizer.

Step 13. Machine buttonhole-stitch around each antenna shape using black thread to complete the top.

Step 14. Finish the quilt referring to the Finishing Instructions on page 173.

NURSERY ORGANIZER

COMPLETING THE TOP
Note: *One Worm Head and two Worm Body blocks and two P-Q units were set aside from making the quilt to complete the Nursery Organizer.*

FABRIC FOR ORGANIZER Measurements based on 43" usable fabric width.	#STRIPS & PIECES	CUT	#PIECES	SUBCUT
⅛ yard red tonal	1	2" x 43"	4	2" K squares
½ yard dark blue tonal	1	14" x 43"	2	15½" F strips
½ yard dark green tonal	1	2" x 43"	2	20" I strips
	2	2" x 24½" J		
	3	2¼" x 43" binding		
⅞ yard cream tonal	1	24½" x 43"	1	6½" B strip
			1	8" C strip
			1	11" G strip
			1	2" H strip
			1	2½" x 15½" E strip
			2	2" x 15½" D strips
			2	2" x 6½" A strips
Backing		33" x 29"		

SUPPLIES
- Batting 33" x 29"
- All-purpose thread to match fabrics
- Quilting thread
- 2 white plastic hanging rings
- 2¾ yards ⅛"-wide blue ribbon
- 26"-long ¼" dowel (optional)
- Basic sewing tools and supplies

Step 1. Join one Worm Head and two Worm Body blocks with two P-Q units and two A strips to make the worm unit as shown in Figure 14; press seams away from blocks.

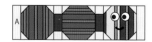

A

Figure 14

Step 2. Sew B to the top of the worm unit; press with seam toward B. Turn B to the wrong side to line the worm unit for worm pocket; press and stitch ¼" from top edge.

Step 3. Place the worm pocket unit on C, aligning sides and bottom; machine-baste along sides and bottom edge to hold. Machine-stitch in the ditch of seams to make pockets as shown in Figure 15.

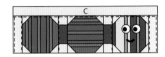

Figure 15

Step 4. Join one E and two each D and F pieces to make the bottom pocket unit as shown in Figure 16; press seams toward D and E pieces.

Figure 16

Step 5. Fold the D-E-F unit in half to make a double layer; press and topstitch ¼" from the folded edge as shown in Figure 17.

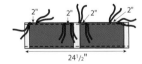

Figure 17

Step 6. Cut eight 12" lengths of ribbon. Fold each length in half and stitch to F as shown in Figure 18 to make ties.

Figure 18

Step 7. Fold the F sections to overlap about 1" as shown in Figure 19 to make pleats. The pleated strip should measure 24½". Machine-baste a scant ¼" from bottom raw edge to form the pocket front.

Figure 19

Step 8. Place the pocket front on the G piece, aligning raw edges; topstitch on each side of the pockets as shown in Figure 20.

Figure 20

Step 9. Sew the H strip to the bottom edge; press seam toward H.

Step 10. Sew the worm pocket to the top of the G/ pleated pocket unit; press seam toward G.

Step 11. Sew I strips to opposite short sides; press seams toward I strips.

Step 12. Sew a K square to each end of each J strip; press seams toward J. Sew the J-K strips to the top and bottom of the pieced unit to complete the pieced top.

Step 13. Arrange and fuse antenna pieces just under Worm Head block and up over C and J; stitch as for Worm Head blocks in quilt.

Step 14. Finish organizer referring to the Finishing Instructions on page 173.

Step 15. Sew two plastic rings to the top back edge for hanging. ***Note:*** *You may add a sleeve to the top back side to insert a small dowel for more secure hanging.*

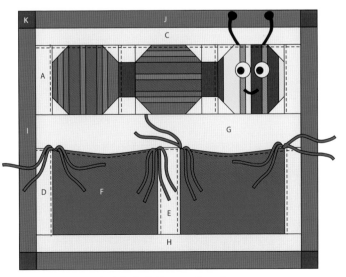

Inch by Inch Nursery Organizer
Placement Diagram 27" x 22½"

COMPLETING THE BUMPER PAD TOPS

Step 1. Join two G strips with one each H, I and J strips with right sides together along length to complete an H-I-J strip set as shown in Figure 21; press seams in one direction. Repeat to make two H-I-J strip sets.

Step 2. Subcut the H-I-J strip sets into (18) 2½" H-I-J units, again referring to Figure 21.

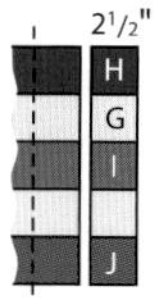

Figure 21 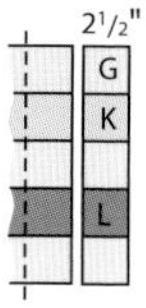   **Figure 22**

Step 3. Join one each K and L strip with three G strips with right sides together along length to make a K-L strip set referring to Figure 22; press seams in one direction.

Step 4. Subcut the K-L strip set into (15) 2½" K-L units, again referring to Figure 22.

Step 5. Join one K-L unit with two H-I-J units to make an X unit as shown in Figure 23; repeat to make three X units. Press seams in one direction.

Figure 23   **Figure 24**

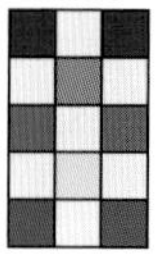

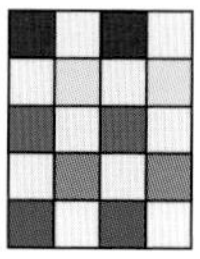

Step 6. Join two K-L units with two H-I-J units to make a Y unit as shown in Figure 24; repeat to make six Y units. Press seams in one direction.

Step 7. Join one each A and E, two each C and D and three B strips to make a strip set as shown in Figure 25; press seams in one direction. Repeat to make three strip sets.

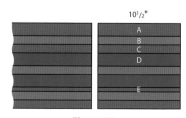

Figure 25

BUMPER PAD

FABRIC FOR BUMPER PAD Measurements based on 43" usable fabric width.	#STRIPS & PIECES	CUT	#PIECES	SUBCUT
⅛ yard red tonal	2	2½" x 43" H		
⅛ yard yellow tonal	1	2½" x 43" K		
⅛ yard orange tonal	1	2½" x 43" L		
½ yard dark aqua tonal	9	1½" x 43" B		
⅝ yard dark blue tonal	6 2	2" x 43" D 2½" x 43" J		
¾ yard dark green tonal	3 6 3 2	2" x 43" A 1½" x 43" C 1" x 43" E 2½" x 43" I		
3¼ yards cream tonal	7 3 12 6	2½" x 43" G 2½" x 43" 1" x 43" 11½" x 27½" O	36 12 12	2½" F squares 27½" N strips 10½" M strips

SUPPLIES
- Neutral color all-purpose thread
- 6—10" x 26" x 1" foam rectangles
- 8 yards ⅛"-wide green satin ribbon
- Basic sewing tools and supplies

Step 8. Subcut the strip sets into nine 10½" stripe units, again referring to Figure 25.

Step 9. Mark a line from corner to corner on the wrong side of each F square.

Step 10. Place F right sides together on each corner of the stripe units as shown in Figure 26; stitch on the marked lines, trim seam allowance to ¼" and press F to the right side to complete nine Stripe blocks, again referring to Figure 26.

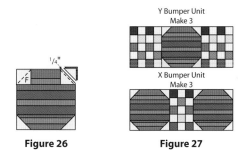

Figure 26

Y Bumper Unit
Make 3

X Bumper Unit
Make 3

Figure 27

Step 11. Join two Y units with one Stripe block to make one Y bumper unit as shown in Figure 27; press seams away from the block. Repeat to make three Y bumper units.

Step 12. Join two Stripe blocks with one X unit to complete an X bumper unit, again referring to Figure 27; press seams away from the blocks. Repeat to make three X bumper units.

Step 13. Sew an M strip to each end and N strips to the top and bottom of each X and Y bumper unit to complete the bumper tops; press seams toward M and N strips.

COMPLETING THE BUMPER PAD

Step 1. Cut ribbon into (24) 12" lengths.

Step 2. Fold a 12" length of ribbon in half and pin to each bumper unit side about 1½" from top and bottom edges as shown in Figure 28.

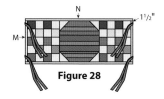

Figure 28

Step 3. Pin an O piece right sides together with each bumper top; stitch all around, catching ribbon folds in stitching, leaving a 6" opening on one side.

Step 4. Turn right side out through opening; press edges flat at seams. Insert foam pieces into each bumper pad through openings.

Step 5. Turn seam allowance in openings to the inside; hand-stitch openings closed to complete six bumper pads.

Step 6. Fit pads into crib and tie ribbons tightly together and to the crib to complete the bumper pad.

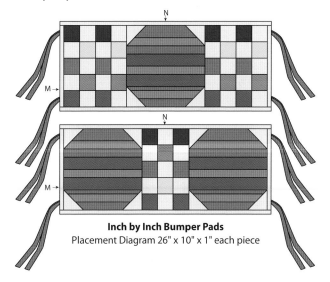

Inch by Inch Bumper Pads
Placement Diagram 26" x 10" x 1" each piece

VALANCE

COMPLETING THE VALANCE

Step 1. Join one each A, C, D, E and F squares with five B squares to make a B unit as shown in Figure 29; press seams in one direction. Repeat to make three B units.

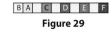

Figure 29

Step 2. Join the B units on the short ends and add a B square to the F end to make a B strip, keeping the same color order.

Step 3. Join the G strips on short ends to make one long strip; press seams to one side. Subcut strip into two 62½" G strips.

Step Instructions

Step 4. Sew a G strip to opposite long sides of the B unit; press seams toward G strips.

Step 5. Join the H strips on short ends to make one long strip; press seams to one side. Subcut strip into one 62½" H strip.

Step 6. Repeat Step 5 with I strips.

Step 7. Sew the I strip to the top and the H strip to the bottom of the pieced unit to complete the valance top; press seams toward I and H strips.

Step 8. Place two J tab strips right sides together and stitch across one end and along both long sides as shown in Figure 30; clip corners and turn right side out. Press edges flat at seams to complete one tab; repeat to make five tabs.

Figure 30

Step 9. Evenly space and pin the tabs along the I edge of the pieced valance top with right sides together and raw edges even; machine-baste to hold in place.

Step 10. Place the lining piece right sides together and join on short ends; press seam open. Trim pieced lining to 62½" long.

Step 11. Place the lining piece right sides together with the pieced valance top; stitch all around, leaving a 6" opening on one end.

Step 12. Turn right side out through opening; press flat at seam edges. Turn seam allowance at opening edges to the inside; hand-stitch opening closed.

Step 13. Fold tabs down even with the bottom of the I strips; pin to hold. Center and hand-stitch a bright-colored button ½" from the bottom of the tabs to complete the valance. ●

FABRIC FOR VALANCE Measurements based on 43" usable fabric width.	#STRIPS & PIECES	CUT	#PIECES	SUBCUT
⅛ yard yellow tonal	3	2½" A squares		
⅛ yard orange tonal	3	2½" C squares		
⅛ yard red tonal	3	2½" F squares		
½ yard blue tonal	3	2½" D squares		
	2	4½" x 43" H		
⅝ yard cream tonal	1	2½" x 43"	16	2½" B squares
	3	4½" x 43" G		
1 yard green tonal	3	2½" E squares		
	2	4½" x 43" I		
	2	4½" x 43"	10	10½" J pieces
1⅛ yards muslin	2	16½" x 43" lining		

SUPPLIES

- Neutral color all-purpose thread
- 5 (1¼") bright-colored round buttons
- Basic sewing tools and supplies

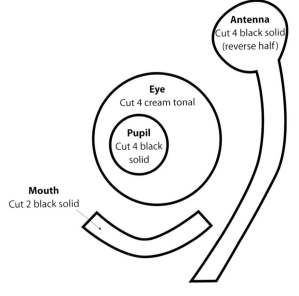

Antenna
Cut 4 black solid
(reverse half)

Eye
Cut 4 cream tonal

Pupil
Cut 4 black solid

Mouth
Cut 2 black solid

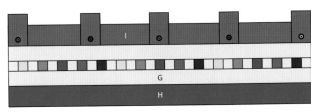

Inch by Inch Valance
Placement Diagram 62" x 16" (without tabs)

Scrappin' Jack

Designs by Julie Higgins

This scrappy baby quilt comes with a happy little Jack perched on his quilted music box.

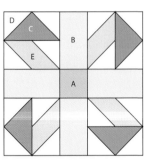

Jack-in-the-Box
10" x 10" Block
Make 9

PROJECT SPECIFICATIONS

Skill Level: Intermediate
Quilt Size: 43" x 43"
Jack/Music Box Size:
5" x 14" x 5"
Block Size: 10" x 10"
Number of Blocks: 9

QUILT

COMPLETING THE BLOCKS

Step 1. Select four same color-family C and E pieces and four same-fabric B pieces for one block.

Step 2. Mark a diagonal line from corner to corner on the wrong side of each D square.

Step 3. To piece one Jack-in-the-Box block, place a D square on one end of C and stitch on the marked line as shown in Figure 1; trim seam to ¼" and press D to the right side, again referring to Figure 1.

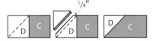

Figure 1

Step 4. Repeat Step 3 with a second D square on the remaining end of C to complete a C-D unit as shown in Figure 2; repeat to make four C-D units.

Figure 2

FABRIC FOR QUILT Measurements based on 42" usable fabric width.	#STRIPS & PIECES	CUT	#PIECES	SUBCUT
⅛ yard each yellow/white, green/white and blue/white stripes	1	2½" x 42" each	8	4½" E pieces each
⅛ yard each blue, yellow and green florals	1	2½" x 42" each	8	4½" C pieces each
⅛ yard blue leaf tonal	1	2½" x 42"	8 1	4½" B pieces 2½" A square
¼ yard yellow leaf tonal	2	2½" x 42"	12 4	4½" B pieces 2½" A squares
¼ yard pink/white stripe	2	2½" x 42"	12	4½" E pieces
¼ yard pink floral	2	2½" x 42"	12	4½" C pieces
⅝ yard pink leaf tonal	2 5	2½" x 42" 2¼" x 42" binding	8 2 4	4½" B pieces 2½" A squares 2½" G squares
¾ yard cream print	9	2½" x 42"	144	2½" D squares
1 yard green leaf tonal	4 4	2½" x 42" 5" x 42" H/I	8 2 12	4½" B pieces 2½" A squares 10½" F strips
Backing		49" x 49"		

SUPPLIES

- Batting 49" x 49"
- Neutral color all-purpose thread
- Quilting thread
- Basic sewing tools and supplies

Step 5. Repeat Steps 3 and 4 with D and E except change the positioning of D to create four D-E units referring to Figure 3.

Figure 3   **Figure 4**

Step 6. Join one C-D unit with one D-E unit to complete a block quarter as shown in Figure 4; press seam toward the D-E unit. Repeat to make four block quarters.

Step 7. Join two block quarters with B to make a row as shown in Figure 5; press seams toward B. Repeat to make two rows.

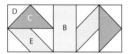

Figure 5   **Figure 6**

Step 8. Join two B pieces with A to make the center row as shown in Figure 6; press seams toward B.

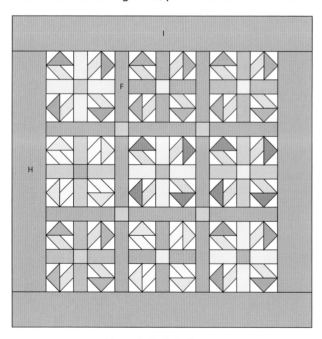

Scrappin' Jack Quilt
Placement Diagram 43" x 43"

Step 9. Sew the rows to the center row referring to the block drawing to complete one Jack-in-the-Box block; press seams toward the center row. Repeat to make nine blocks, keeping the C and E pieces in the same color family in each block and using four matching B pieces. Refer to the Placement Diagram for placement of colors in each block.

COMPLETING THE QUILT

Step 1. Join three Jack-in-the-Box blocks with two F pieces to complete a block row; press seams toward F pieces. Repeat to make three block rows.

Step 2. Join three F pieces with two G squares to make a sashing row as shown in Figure 7; press seams toward G squares. Repeat to make two sashing rows.

Figure 7

Step 3. Join the block rows with the sashing rows referring to the Placement Diagram for positioning of rows; press seams toward sashing rows.

Step 4. Join the H-I strips on short ends to make one long strip; press seams open. Subcut strip into two 34½" H strips and two 43½" I strips.

Step 5. Sew H strips to opposite sides and I strips to the top and bottom of the pieced center; press seams toward H and I strips.

Step 5. Finish the quilt referring to the Finishing Instructions on page 173.

SCRAPPIN' JACK MUSIC BOX

COMPLETING THE BOX BASE

Step 1. Trace the heart shape onto the scrap of fusible web; cut out shape, leaving a margin all around.

Step 2. Fuse shape to the wrong side of the pink floral; cut out shape on traced line. Remove paper backing.

Step 3. Center and fuse the heart shape on the green J square.

FABRIC FOR MUSIC BOX Measurements based on 42" usable fabric width.	#STRIPS & PIECES	CUT	#PIECES	SUBCUT
Assorted pink, yellow, blue and green tonal, floral and stripe scraps		Yo-yo pieces as per patterns		
¼ yard yellow leaf tonal	1	6½" x 6½" J Yo-yo pieces as per patterns		
¼ yard yellow/white stripe	1	6½" x 6½" J Yo-yo pieces as per patterns		
¼ yard blue leaf tonal	2	6½" x 6½" J Yo-yo pieces as per patterns		
¼ yard pink floral		Heart as per pattern Yo-yo pieces as per patterns		
¼ yard peach solid		Head and hand pieces as per patterns		
¼ yard each pink/white and blue/white plaids		Hat pieces as per pattern		
¼ yard lining fabric	1	6½" x 42"	5 2	6½" J lining squares 4" K lining pieces
½ yard green leaf tonal	1	6½" x 42"	1 2	6½" J square 4" K pieces
		Body and shoe pieces as per patterns Yo-yo pieces as per patterns		

SUPPLIES

- Thin batting 4—6½" x 6½" J and 2—6½" x 4" K
- All-purpose thread to match fabrics
- Quilting thread
- Button thread to match fabrics
- 12" (¾"-wide) ruffled lace
- Copper-colored eyelash yarn
- Polyester fiberfill
- 3½" square fusible web
- Black and brown extra-fine permanent pens
- Light and dark rose crayons
- Medium and dark green, white and tan fabric paints or markers
- 3" doll needle
- Freezer paper
- Small windup music box
- Basic sewing tools and supplies

Step 4. Pin the scrap of fabric stabilizer to the wrong side of the fused square. Machine zigzag-stitch around the heart shape using thread to match fabric; remove fabric stabilizer when stitching is complete.

Step 5. Layer a batting J square between the appliquéd J square and one lining J square; pin layers together to hold flat. Repeat with remaining four J squares.

Step 6. Machine-quilt a meandering pattern over each layered J unit; trim the quilted squares to 5½" x 5½", centering the heart shape on the appliquéd square.

Step 7. Repeat Steps 5 and 6 with the K pieces and trim to 5½" x 3".

Step 8. Join the two K rectangles on the 5½" sides, leaving 3" open in the center. *Note: The opening will be used to turn the box right side out, stuff and insert the music box.*

Step 9. With right sides together, stitch the yellow J units and the appliquéd unit together with the K unit, stopping and starting stitching ¼" from the edge of each piece as shown in Figure 8, and securing stitching at the beginning and end of each seam.

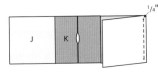

Figure 8

Step 10. Insert and stitch the top and bottom J units to make a box as shown in Figure 9.

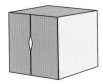

Figure 9

Step 11. Turn the box right side out through the opening in the K unit; stuff box firmly, but before finishing, insert the music box into the opening. Finish stuffing around the box and hand-stitch the opening closed on each side of the windup key, leaving the key protruding, to finish.

COMPLETING THE DOLL BODY

Step 1. Trace body, shoe and hand patterns given onto freezer paper. Cut large enough pieces of fabric to fit generously around the templates.

Step 2. Layer two pieces of fabric to be sewn right sides together and iron freezer-paper shapes onto one wrong side; do not cut out.

Step 3. Set machine for a short stitch length; use the freezer-paper template as a guide as you sew around the edge, leaving an opening to turn right side out referring to Figure 10 and pattern pieces. *Note: The edge of the template is the seam line; remember to leave openings where indicated for turning the piece.*

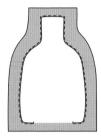

Figure 10

Step 4. After stitching around each piece, trim close to stitching line, clipping curves and points as necessary.

Step 5. Remove the freezer-paper shapes; turn right side out through openings.

Step 6. Trace head shape onto the wrong side of head fabric twice; cut out each, adding a ¼" seam allowance all around.

Step 7. Center and trace face on right side of one head. Use brown permanent pen to trace over lines again. Referring to photo, add color as follows: Use light and dark rose crayons to color lips, using light shade to highlight bottom lip. Shade cheeks slightly with light rose crayon. With medium and dark green fabric paints or markers color in iris, using darker shade right under the eyelid. Shade eyelid with tan. Use black permanent pen to make pupil in center of iris, and to darken eye lines and lashes as desired. Place a tiny dot of white paint next to each pupil for highlight. Let paints dry completely.

Step 8. Place head pieces right sides together and stitch on marked lines, leaving neck end open for turning. Turn right side out; stuff firmly, shaping head as you stuff.

Step 9. Stuff stitched body firmly; hand-stitch opening on bottom closed.

Step 10. Push the neck firmly up into the head opening; attach head to body. Stitch a second time to secure.

Step 11. Stuff stitched hand pieces slightly; stitch along finger lines as marked on pattern. Add more stuffing above stitched fingers; sew hand openings closed.

Step 12. Stuff shoes firmly; stitch openings closed.

Step 13. Using eyelash yarn, wrap strands around three fingers about 7 or 8 times, making a loop. Securely attach the loop to the head starting at the front and working toward the back. Repeat to make as many loops as necessary to fill in hair, slightly fluffing yarn as you go.

Step 14. Cut hat pieces as directed on pattern; place right sides together. Stitch side edges and points, stitching just to seam allowance dots at top and bottom of points as shown in Figure 11. Turn right side out; turn bottom raw edges to the inside and hand-stitch to close. Hand-stitch side edges together as shown in Figure 12. Tack hat to the doll's head.

Figure 11   **Figure 12**

COMPLETING THE MUSIC BOX

Step 1. Turn under the edge of each yo-yo circle ¼", hand-stitch ⅛" from edge and pull thread to gather to complete one yo-yo as shown in Figure 13; secure ends. Repeat to make 22 small and 24 large yo-yos.

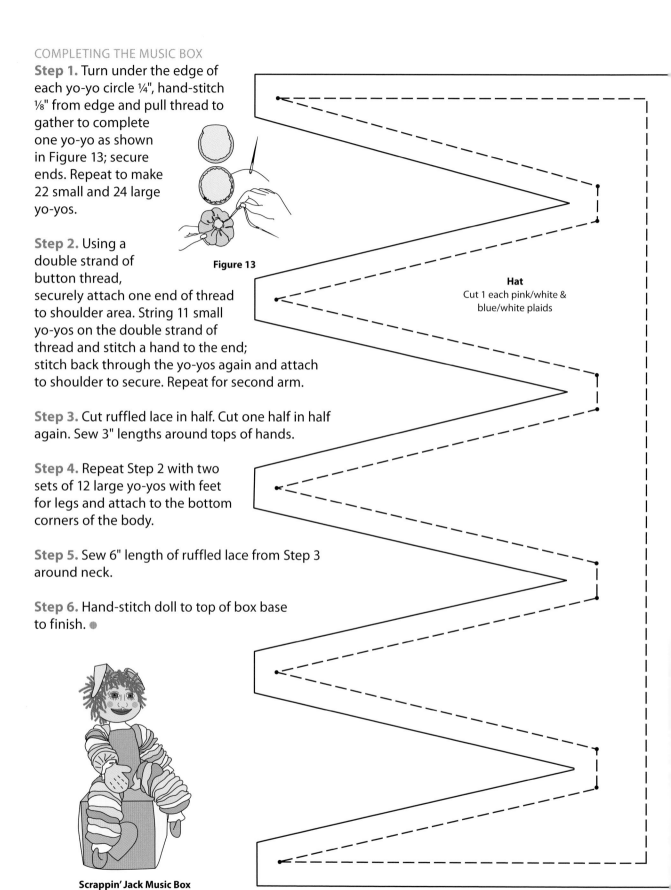

Figure 13

Step 2. Using a double strand of button thread, securely attach one end of thread to shoulder area. String 11 small yo-yos on the double strand of thread and stitch a hand to the end; stitch back through the yo-yos again and attach to shoulder to secure. Repeat for second arm.

Step 3. Cut ruffled lace in half. Cut one half in half again. Sew 3" lengths around tops of hands.

Step 4. Repeat Step 2 with two sets of 12 large yo-yos with feet for legs and attach to the bottom corners of the body.

Step 5. Sew 6" length of ruffled lace from Step 3 around neck.

Step 6. Hand-stitch doll to top of box base to finish. ●

Hat
Cut 1 each pink/white & blue/white plaids

Scrappin' Jack Music Box
Placement Diagram 5" x 14" x 5"

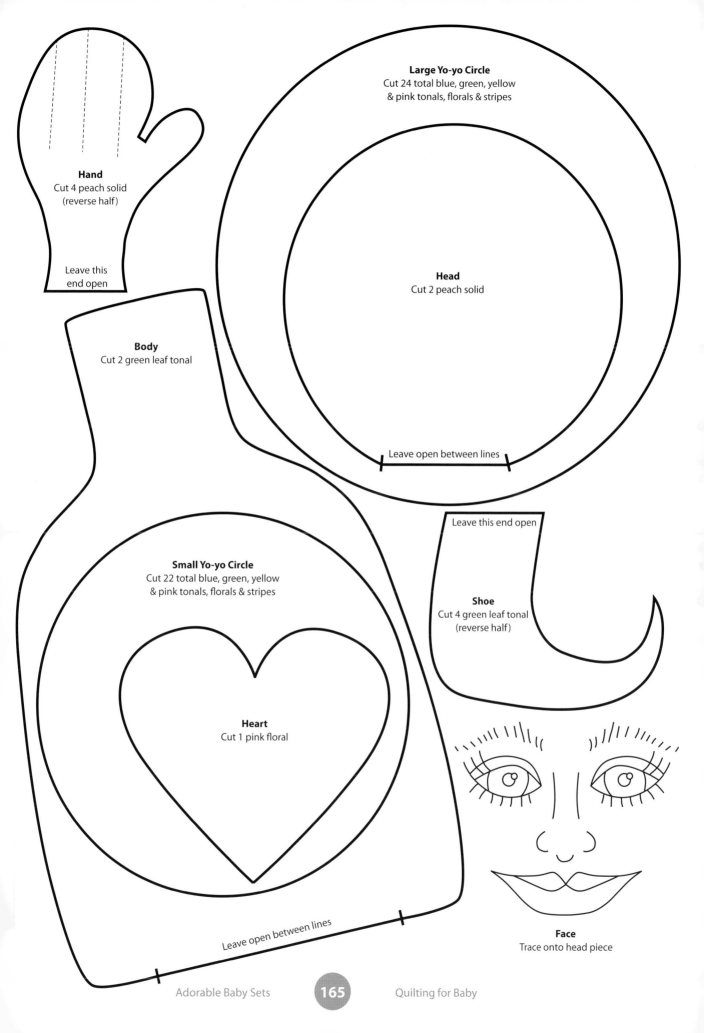

Hand
Cut 4 peach solid
(reverse half)

Leave this
end open

Large Yo-yo Circle
Cut 24 total blue, green, yellow
& pink tonals, florals & stripes

Head
Cut 2 peach solid

Leave open between lines

Body
Cut 2 green leaf tonal

Leave this end open

Shoe
Cut 4 green leaf tonal
(reverse half)

Small Yo-yo Circle
Cut 22 total blue, green, yellow
& pink tonals, florals & stripes

Heart
Cut 1 pink floral

Leave open between lines

Face
Trace onto head piece

Nouveau Baby Quilt & Keeper Board

Designs by Jodi Warner

Try a new color scheme for Baby with a quilt and keeper board to match.

PROJECT SPECIFICATIONS

Skill Level: Intermediate
Quilt Size: 43" x 55"
Keeper Board Size: Approximately 27" x 22" including frame
Block Size: 6" x 6"
Number of Blocks: 35

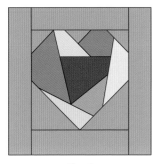

Heart
6" x 6" Block
Make 18

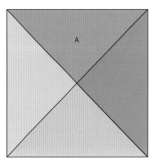

Hourglass
6" x 6" Block
Make 17

QUILT

COMPLETING THE HEART BLOCKS

Note: *Cut pieces for paper piecing from all fabrics as needed. Use assorted fabrics for heart piecing. Use same fabric for Nos. 13, 14, 15 and 16 pieces in one block.*

Step 1. Prepare copies of paper-piecing pattern given. Set machine stitch length to 1.5 or 15 stitches to the inch.

Step 2. To complete one Heart block, place piece 1 in the No. 1 position on the unmarked side of

FABRIC FOR QUILT Measurements based on 43" usable fabric width.	#STRIPS & PIECES	CUT	#PIECES	SUBCUT
Fat quarter each 15–19 prints	1	7½" square each 11 fabrics		Cut on both diagonals to make 44 A triangles
	18	I Sets Nos. 1–12 pieces as per paper piecing pattern		
	18	Pairs 1½" x 4¾" Nos. 13/14 pieces		
	18	Pairs 1½" x 6¾" Nos. 15/16 pieces to match Nos. 13/14 pieces		
½ yard brown dot	2	1½" x 42½" B		
	2	1½" x 32½" C		
	1	7¼" square		Cut on both diagonals to make 4 A triangles
⅝ yard salmon tonal	3	2" x 43" D		
	2	2" x 35½" E		
	1	7¼" square		Cut on both diagonals to make 4 A triangles
⅔ yard light green/ navy dot	5	2¼" x 43" binding		
	2	7¼" squares		Cut on both diagonals to make 8 A triangles
1 yard green/blue plaid	5	4½" x 43" F/G		
	2	7¼" squares		Cut on both diagonals to make 8 A triangles
Backing		49" x 61"		

SUPPLIES

- Batting 49" x 61"
- Neutral color all-purpose thread
- Quilting thread
- Basic sewing tools and supplies

the paper; pin in place. Place piece 2 right sides together with piece 1; stitch on the 1-2 line on the marked side of the paper as shown in Figure 1.

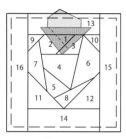

Figure 1   **Figure 2**

Step 3. Press piece 2 to the right side; fold back and trim the 1-2 fabric seam to ¼" if necessary and as shown in Figure 2. Repeat with pieces 3–16 in numerical order to cover the pattern.

Step 4. Trim the pieced block unit to 6½" x 6½", if necessary; remove paper foundation.

Step 5. Repeat Steps 2–4 to complete 18 Heart blocks.

COMPLETING THE HOURGLASS BLOCKS
Step 1. Select four different A triangles.

Step 2. Join two A triangles on short sides to make an A unit as shown in Figure 3; press seam in one direction. Repeat to make two A units, pressing seams in opposite directions.

Figure 3

Step 3. Join the two A units to complete one Hourglass block referring to the block drawing; press seam in one direction.

Step 4. Repeat Steps 1–3 to complete 17 Hourglass blocks.

COMPLETING THE QUILT
Step 1. Join three Heart blocks with two Hourglass blocks to make an X row as shown in Figure 4; press seams toward Hourglass blocks. Repeat to make four X rows.

Step 2. Join three Hourglass blocks with two Heart blocks to make a Y row, again referring to Figure 4; press seams toward the Hourglass blocks. Repeat to make three Y rows.

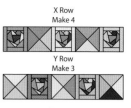

Figure 4

Step 3. Join the X and Y rows referring to the Placement Diagram for positioning; press seams in one direction.

Step 4. Sew a B strip to opposite long sides and C strips to the top and bottom of the pieced center; press seams toward B and C strips.

Step 5. Join the D strips on short ends to make one long strip; press seams open. Subcut strip into two 44½" D strips.

Step 6. Sew a D strip to opposite long sides and E strips to the top and bottom of the pieced center to complete the pieced top; press seams toward D and E strips.

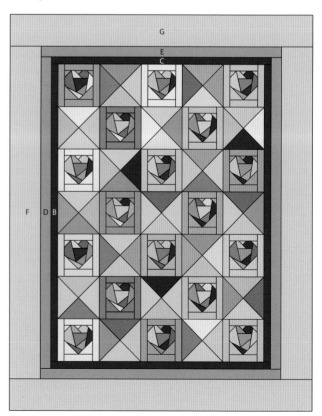

Nouveau Baby Quilt
Placement Diagram 43" x 55"

Step 7. Join the F/G strips on short ends to make one long strip; press seams open. Subcut strip into two 47½" F strips and two 43½" G strips.

Step 8. Sew an F strip to opposite long sides and G strips to the top and bottom of the pieced center to complete the pieced top; press seams toward F and G strips.

Step 9. Finish the quilt referring to the Finishing Instructions on page 173. ***Note:*** *The swirling star quilting design given was quilted in the borders and the heart quilting design was quilted in the center of each Heart block.*

KEEPER BOARD

FABRIC FOR KEEPER BOARD Measurements based on 43" usable fabric width.	#STRIPS & PIECES	CUT
14—8½" x 9" scraps		Refer to patterns for cutting
▨ Green scrap	3	1¼" diameter circles

SUPPLIES

- Thin batting 23" x 17"
- All-purpose thread to match fabrics
- Ready-made corkboard with narrow wooden frame and 23" x 17" cork area
- 4 yards ½"–¾"-wide white grosgrain ribbon
- 1⅜ yards 1¼"–2"-wide wire-edge dark brown grosgrain ribbon
- 3 (½") or larger thumbtacks
- Fray preventative
- Template material
- Optional: wooden door molding, cut to size with mitered corners and glued to frame edges
- Optional: 4 screw-hold mushroom plugs
- Contrasting acrylic paint and paintbrush
- Clear quick-drying fabric glue
- Temporary pencil or masking tape
- Clear topcoat protective spray
- Basic sewing tools and supplies

COMPLETING THE KEEPER BOARD TOP

Step 1. Prepare templates H and I using patterns given; cut as directed on each piece. ***Note:*** *Please note that the outer edge seam allowances of H and I pieces are ⅜" and are included in the template.*

Step 2. Join five H and one each I and IR pieces as shown in Figure 5; press seams open. Repeat to make two H-I rows.

Figure 5

Step 3. Join the two H-I rows using a ⅜" seam allowance to complete the pieced top as shown in Figure 6; press seams open.

Figure 6

COMPLETING THE KEEPER BOARD FRAME

Note: *Adding the patchwork top to the corkboard will be easier if there is a little space between the cork and the frame.*

Step 1. Cut, glue and sand optional wooden door molding at outer corkboard edges.

Step 2. Mark and drill optional screw holes and/or mushroom plug holes. ***Note:*** *Check hanging location and studs or anchor applications and space holes accordingly.*

Step 3. Mask off cork area; paint wooden frame front and edge surfaces with acrylic paint. Paint optional mushroom plugs with contrasting acrylic paint. Finish all with clear topcoat protective spray.

PATCHWORK TOP INSERTION

Step 1. Mark opening side centers on frame with temporary pencil or masking tape.

Step 2. Cut the thin batting rectangle to size slightly smaller than the exposed cork area. Glue in place at edges and across horizontal center; allow to dry.

Step 3. Position and pin the pieced top in place along top and bottom edges, aligning horizontal seam with center marks on frame.

Step 4. Apply clear glue between fabric layer and batting slightly away from frame edges; allow to dry. Use thin edge such as credit card to gently but firmly push the raw edge of the pieced top under the edge of the frame. ***Note:*** *If the corkboard does not allow enough space between frame opening and cork layer for tucking edge of fabric under before gluing fabric in place, neatly turn edges under to create a fold flush with wooden frame. Position and glue grosgrain ribbon in place before turning edges under (see next step).*

Step 5. Position grosgrain ribbon, crossing strips over patchwork seams referring to Figure 7 and cut to size, allowing ⅜" to extend beyond frame edge; glue each strip in place near frame edge and at center crossings only. Push excess under frame edge as in Step 4.

Figure 7

COMPLETING THE ROSETTES
Step 1. Cut wire-edge ribbon into three 14½"–15" lengths.

Step 2. Fold (15) ¼" pleats in each length of ribbon as shown in Figure 8 (length should now measure approximately 4½").

I
Cut 4 scraps
(reverse 2 for IR)

Figure 8   **Figure 9**

Step 3. Machine-baste ¾" from inside edge; trim excess off a scant ¼" beyond basting. Overlap ends so that pleating is continued as shown in Figure 9, then place right sides together and sew along ends; trim excess.

Step 4. With hand-sewing needle and matching thread, anchor and gather-stitch around rosette center near basting (catching only pleat fold edges onto needle and thread) as shown in Figure 10, cinching in while stitching, until rosette diameter measures approximately 1¾"; tie off securely.

Figure 10

Step 5. Apply fray preventative to raw ribbon seam edges and cut edges at center; allow to dry.

Step 6. For centers, cut a batting circle to match the size of the large thumbtack head and glue in place.

Step 7. With hand-sewing needle and matching thread, anchor and gather-stitch around each 1¼" fabric circle ⅛" in from raw edge as shown in Figure 11. Place thumbtack head on the wrong side of fabric circle and cinch up tightly, again referring to Figure 11; secure and tie off.

Figure 11

Step 8. Apply glue to the front center of the rosette; insert tack point through center. Allow to dry.

Step 9. Apply glue to the three ribbon/seam intersections on board; insert tack point through fabric panel into cork and allow to dry.

Step 10. Mount keeper board as desired. To use, pin message through fabric into the cork, or slide edge of card, list or note under ribbon strips. ●

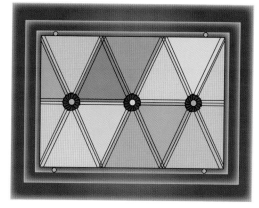

Nouveau Keeper Board
Placement Diagram Approximately 27" x 22" (including frame)

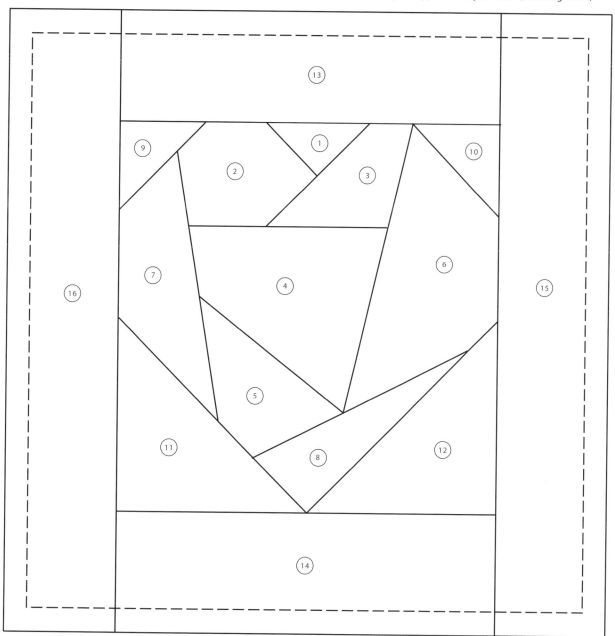

Paper-Piecing Pattern
Make 18 copies

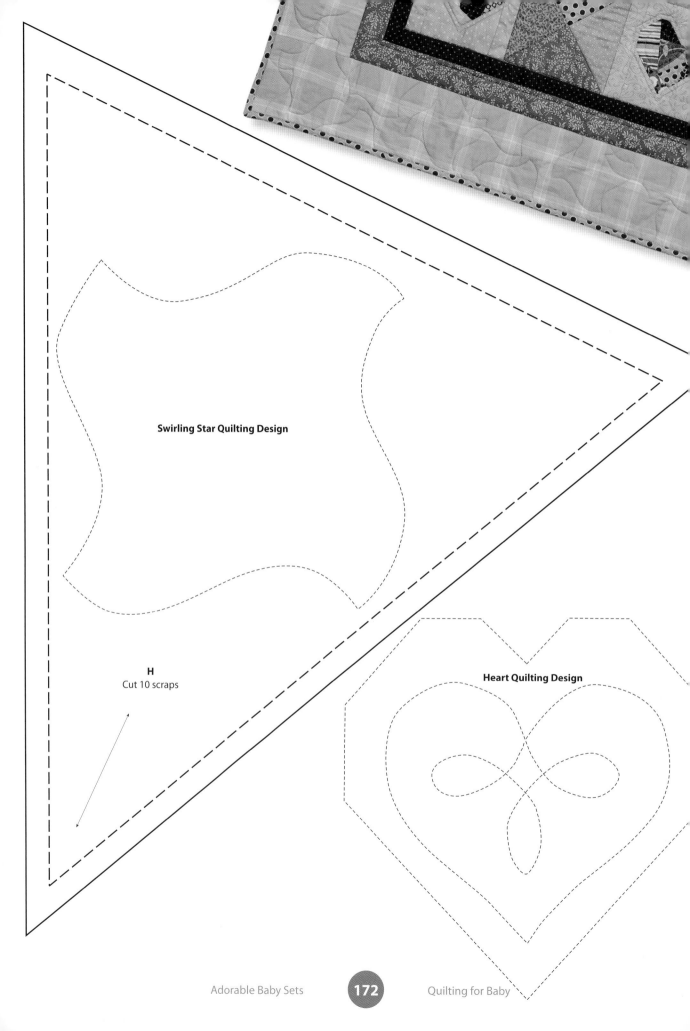

Swirling Star Quilting Design

H
Cut 10 scraps

Heart Quilting Design

Finishing Instructions

When you have completed the quilt top as instructed with patterns, finish your quilt with these four easy steps.

Step 1. Sandwich the batting between the completed top and prepared backing; pin or baste layers together to hold. *Note: If using basting spray to hold layers together, refer to instructions on the product container for use.*

Step 2. Quilt as desired by hand or machine; remove pins or basting. Trim excess backing and batting even with quilt top.

Step 3. Join binding strips on short ends to make one long strip. Fold the strip in half along length with wrong sides together; press.

Step 4. Sew binding to quilt edges, mitering corners and overlapping ends. Fold binding to the back side and stitch in place to finish. ●

Metric Conversion Charts

Metric Conversions

yards	x	.9144	=	metres (m)
yards	x	91.44	=	centimetres (cm)
inches	x	2.54	=	centimetres (cm)
inches	x	25.40	=	millimetres (mm)
inches	x	.0254	=	metres (m)

centimetres	x	.3937	=	inches
metres	x	1.0936	=	yards

Standard Equivalents

⅛ inch	=	3.20 mm	=	0.32 cm
¼ inch	=	6.35 mm	=	0.635 cm
⅜ inch	=	9.50 mm	=	0.95 cm
½ inch	=	12.70 mm	=	1.27 cm
⅝ inch	=	15.90 mm	=	1.59 cm
¾ inch	=	19.10 mm	=	1.91 cm
⅞ inch	=	22.20 mm	=	2.22 cm
1 inch	=	25.40 mm	=	2.54 cm
⅛ yard	=	11.43 cm	=	0.11 m
¼ yard	=	22.86 cm	=	0.23 m
⅜ yard	=	34.29 cm	=	0.34 m
½ yard	=	45.72 cm	=	0.46 m
⅝ yard	=	57.15 cm	=	0.57 m
¾ yard	=	68.58 cm	=	0.69 m
⅞ yard	=	80.00 cm	=	0.80 m
1 yard	=	91.44 cm	=	0.91 m

1⅛ yard	=	102.87 cm	=	1.03 m
1¼ yard	=	114.30 cm	=	1.14 m
1⅜ yard	=	125.73 cm	=	1.26 m
1½ yard	=	137.16 cm	=	1.37 m
1⅝ yard	=	148.59 cm	=	1.49 m
1¾ yard	=	160.02 cm	=	1.60 m
1⅞ yard	=	171.44 cm	=	1.71 m
2 yards	=	182.88 cm	=	1.83 m
2⅛ yards	=	194.31 cm	=	1.94 m
2¼ yards	=	205.74 cm	=	2.06 m
2⅜ yards	=	217.17 cm	=	2.17 m
2½ yards	=	228.60 cm	=	2.29 m
2⅝ yards	=	240.03 cm	=	2.40 m
2¾ yards	=	251.46 cm	=	2.51 m
2⅞ yards	=	262.88 cm	=	2.63 m
3 yards	=	274.32 cm	=	2.74 m
3⅛ yards	=	285.75 cm	=	2.86 m
3¼ yards	=	297.18 cm	=	2.97 m
3⅜ yards	=	308.61 cm	=	3.09 m
3½ yards	=	320.04 cm	=	3.20 m
3⅝ yards	=	331.47 cm	=	3.31 m
3¾ yards	=	342.90 cm	=	3.43 m
3⅞ yards	=	354.32 cm	=	3.54 m
4 yards	=	365.76 cm	=	3.66 m
4⅛ yards	=	377.19 cm	=	3.77 m
4¼ yards	=	388.62 cm	=	3.89 m
4⅜ yards	=	400.05 cm	=	4.00 m
4½ yards	=	411.48 cm	=	4.11 m
4⅝ yards	=	422.91 cm	=	4.23 m
4¾ yards	=	434.34 cm	=	4.34 m
4⅞ yards	=	445.76 cm	=	4.46 m
5 yards	=	457.20 cm	=	4.57 m

Photo Index

Irresistible Baby Quilts

6 Sweet Dreams

10 Under the Sea

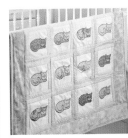
15 Sleepy Kitty Nap Quilt

17 Comfy Corners Play Quilt

20 Fun Fish Quilt

23 Cowboy Stars

26 Simple Six

29 Folded Four-Patch Play Quilt

32 Let's Play Peekaboo

36 Lavender Lullaby

40 Sunshine & Ribbons

44 Pooches & Patches

48 Spring Bright Baby Quilt

52 Just Ducky Baby Quilt

56 Crazy-Patch Safari

Fun Baby Accessories

Adorable Baby Sets

Special Thanks

Please join us in thanking the talented designers listed below for their work.

Ann Anderson
Sunshine & Ribbons, 40

Mary Ayres
Fun Fish Quilt, 20
Little Lamb Bib &
Burp Pad, 68
Teddy Bear Frame, 119

Barbara Clayton
Ducks Around the World, 140

Jenny Foltz
Hugs & Kisses Play Quilt, 102
Inch by Inch, 151

Sandra L. Hatch
Animal Fun, 126
I Spy Four-Patch, 65

Julie Higgins
Scrappin' Jack, 159

Connie Kauffman
Bright & Charming Baby, 146
Flower Fancies, 132
Lavender Lullaby, 36
Peekaboo Monkeys, 78

Mary Kerr
Just Ducky Baby Quilt, 52

Susan Knapp
Let's Play Peekaboo, 32

Chris Malone
Cute as a Button, 83
Denim All-Boy Tote, 74
Little Lamb Baby Quilt, 98

Barbara Miller
Crazy-Patch Safari, 56

Linda Miller
Comfy Corners Play Quilt, 17

Lisa Moore
Cowboy Stars, 23

Sue Harvey & Sandy Boobar
Folded Four-Patch
Play Quilt, 29
Fun Frog Play Mat, 88
Mom's Forever Tote
& Pouch, 93
Simple Six, 26

Connie Rand
Discovery Baby Quilt, 62
Sleepy Kitty Nap Quilt, 15

Jill Reber
Baby Steps Duo, 123
Nursery Quilt & Runner, 136

Nancy Richoux
Pooches & Patches, 44

Christine Schultz
Baby Welcome Wall Quilt, 106
Spring Bright Baby Quilt, 48

Jodi Warner
Stroller Buddy Pack, 112
Nouveau Baby Quilt & Keeper
Board, 166

Julie Weaver
Sweet Dreams, 6
Under the Sea, 10
Whirligigs Changing Mat, 72

Fabric & Supplies

Page 6: Sweet Dreams—Thermore batting from Hobbs

Page 10: Under the Sea—Warm & Natural cotton batting from The Warm Co. and Triangle in a Square ruler from Quilt in a Day.

Page 15: Sleepy Kitty Nap Quilt—Beatrix Potter Alphabet Garden fabric collection from Quilting Treasures, Mountain Mist Cream Rose batting and Star Machine Quilting thread from Coats.

Page 20: Fun Fish Quilt—Warm & White needled cotton batting and Lite Steam-A-Seam fusible web from The Warm Co.

Page 26: Simple Six—Machine 60/40 Blend batting from Fairfield Processing and Star Machine Quilting thread from Coats.

Page 29: Folded Four-Patch Play Quilt—Batik fabrics from Diamond Textiles, Machine 60/40 Blend batting from Fairfield Processing and Star Machine Quilting thread from Coats.

Page 36: Lavender Lullaby—Sulky Rayon threads and Fusible cotton batting from Hobbs.

Page 62: Discovery Baby Quilt—Ladybug Love and Fun Frogs from Blank Quilting, Cream Rose batting from Mountain Mist and Star Machine Quilting thread from Coats.

Page 65: I Spy Four-Patch Quilt—Eco-Craft Eco-Friendly blend batting from Mountain Mist and Star Machine Quilting thread from Coats. Machine-quilted by Dianne Hodgkins.

Page 68: Little Lamb Bib & Burp Pad—Warm & White needled cotton batting and Steam-A-Seam fusible web from The Warm Co.

Page 72: Whirligigs Changing Mat—Warm & Natural batting from The Warm Co.

Page 78: Peekaboo Monkeys—Blendable thread from Sulky, Fusible cotton batting from Hobbs and Steam-A-Seam2 fusible web from The Warm Co.

Page 88: Fun Frog Play Mat—Machine 60/40 Blend batting from Fairfield Processing and Star Machine Quilting thread from Coats.

Page 112: Stroller Buddy Pack: Timtex

Page 123: Baby Steps Duo—Master Piece 45 ruler and Static Stickers.

Page 126: Animal Fun—Fabric ©Disney: Based on the "Winnie the Pooh" works by A.A. Milne and E.H. Shepard. Visit the Disney Web site at www.disney.com © 2008 Springs Creative Products Group, LLC., Rock Hill, S.C. 29730 www.spring-screative.com. Eco-Craft Eco-Friendly blend batting from Mountain Mist and Star Machine Quilting thread from Coats. Machine-quilted by Dianne Hodgkins.

Page 132: Flower Fancies—Spring Meadows fabric collection from Moda, Steam-A-Seam2 fusible web, Sulky Blendable threads and Sulky KK2000 temporary spray adhesive.

Page 136: Nursery Quilt & Runner—Master Piece 45 ruler and Static Stickers.

Page 146: Bright & Charming Baby—Strawberry Lemonade fabric collection from Moda, Poly/cotton batting from Hobbs and Blendable thread from Sulky.

Page 159: Scrappin' Jack—Clover Large and Extra Large Quick Yo-Yo Makers and Turn it All tool.

Page 166: Nouveau Baby Quilt & Keeper Board—Fray Check fray preventative and Fabric-Tac fabric glue.